ENCOUNTERS WITH THE "HOLY LAND"

PLACE, PAST AND FUTURE IN AMERICAN JEWISH CULTURE

EDITED BY JEFFREY SHANDLER AND BETH S. WENGER

PUBLISHED BY THE NATIONAL MUSEUM OF AMERICAN JEWISH HISTORY;
THE CENTER FOR JUDAIC STUDIES, UNIVERSITY OF PENNSYLVANIA;
AND THE UNIVERSITY OF PENNSYLVANIA LIBRARY
IN ASSOCIATION WITH BRANDEIS UNIVERSITY PRESS
DISTRIBUTED BY UNIVERSITY PRESS OF NEW ENGLAND
HANOVER AND LONDON

This catalogue has been published in conjunction with the exhibition "HOLY LAND": AMERICAN ENCOUNTERS WITH THE LAND OF ISRAEL IN THE CENTURY BEFORE STATEHOOD.
23 January – 5 July 1998

Published by the National Museum of American Jewish History; the Center for Judaic Studies, University of Pennsylvania; and the University of Pennsylvania Library

Distributed by University Press of New England, Hanover, NH 03755

Library of Congress Catalog
Card Number 97-076102

ISBN 1-891507-00-1

Catalogue Design: Greg Bear
Photography: Will Brown
Printing: French Bray, Inc.

Cover Images:
Lithograph of the Wailing Wall from Rev. George Robert Gleig, *Carl Werner's Jerusalem, Bethlehem, and the Holy Places,* London, 1865
Center for Judaic Studies,
University of Pennsylvania Library

International Jewish Arts Festival, Suffolk Y Jewish Community Center, Commack, Long Island, 1995. Copyright Frédéric Brenner/Courtesy of Howard Greenberg Gallery, NY.

Brandeis Series in American Jewish History, Culture, and Life

Jonathan D. Sarna, Editor
Sylvia Barack Fishman, Associate Editor

The Brandeis Series in American Jewish History, Culture, and Life publishes works that encompass all areas of American Jewish civilization, including history, religion, thought, politics, economics, sociology, anthropology, literature and the arts. Of particular interest are interdisciplinary studies that tie together divergent aspects of the American Jewish experience.

The Tauber Institute for the Study of European Jewry Series

Jehuda Reinharz, General Editor
Michael Brenner, Associate Editor

The Tauber Institute for the Study of European Jewry, established by a gift to Brandeis University from Dr. Laszlo N. Tauber, is dedicated to the memory of the victims of Nazi persecutions between 1933 and 1945. The Institute seeks to study the history and culture of European Jewry in the modern period. The Institute has a special interest in studying the causes, nature, and consequences of the European Jewish catastrophe within the contexts of modern European diplomatic, intellectual, political, and social history.

The Jacob and Libby Goodman Institute for the Study of Zionism and Israel is organized under the auspices of the Tauber Institute. The Goodman Institute seeks to promote an understanding of the historical and ideological development of the Zionist movement and the State of Israel.

This book is number 28 in the series.

Jerusalem display, Louisiana Purchase Exposition
St. Louis, Mo., 1904
H.C. White Co.

Contents

6   Foreword

8   Acknowledgments

Essays

11   "The Site of Paradise":
The Holy Land in American Jewish Imagination
by Jeffrey Shandler and Beth S. Wenger

41   Celebrating Zion in America
by Arthur A. Goren

60   A Place in the World:
Jews and the Holy Land at World's Fairs
by Barbara Kirshenblatt-Gimblett

83   Checklist of the Exhibition

104   List of Lenders

Foreword

"HOLY LAND": AMERICAN ENCOUNTERS WITH THE LAND OF ISRAEL IN THE CENTURY BEFORE STATEHOOD began with a discussion between two colleagues about a modest exhibition. In the spring of 1996, David Ruderman and Michael Ryan had the idea to create an exhibition of materials from the collection of the Center for Judaic Studies at the University of Pennsylvania, which Ruderman directs, for display in the Kamin Gallery of the Van Pelt Library on the University campus, where Ryan is the Director of Special Collections.

To that end, Ruderman asked two of the Center's fellows to examine the CJS collection carefully, and propose an exhibition related to the Center's 1996-1997 theme: "Divergent Centers: Israeli and American Jewry in the 20th Century."

Those scholars, Dr. Jeffrey Shandler and Dr. Beth Wenger, soon returned with an exciting and ambitious proposal based on the extraordinary material that they had uncovered, most of which had never been seen by the general public. They suggested an exhibition examining the relationships of Americans, both Jews and non-Jews, to the Land of Israel and how these relationships became critical components of American Jewish identity, both past and present.

Given the embarrassment of riches the two uncovered, and the importance of the subject to understanding American Jewish culture, Ruderman called Margo Bloom, Director of the National Museum of American Jewish History in search of a partner. Such a partnership would not only provide the space and professional competence this topic deserved; it would attract people to both the Museum and the Van Pelt galleries, the two sites where the exhibition would be held. The collaboration would also create a meaningful encounter between two prominent cultural institutions in the Philadelphia community.

The Museum had long been interested in exploring this topic, and had also collected in the area. With the breadth of its own collection, together with that of the Center and other repositories around the country, it was clear that an exhibition would fill the galleries of the National Museum of American Jewish History, and the Kamin Gallery at the Van Pelt Library.

Once this was decided, we had an important deadline to meet. The 50th anniversary of the creation of the state of Israel is marked in 1998. "HOLY LAND": AMERICAN ENCOUNTERS WITH THE LAND OF ISRAEL IN THE CENTURY BEFORE STATEHOOD provided a perfect salute to this landmark occasion.

Shandler, a Dorot Teaching Fellow at the Skirball Department of Hebrew and Judaic Studies at New York University, and Wenger, Katz Family Chair in American Jewish History and Assistant Professor at the University of Pennsylvania, began this project as fellows at the Center, and served as exhibition curators. Shandler and Wenger brought both passion and perception to the organization of a complex topic. Their skill and proficiency as scholars extend not only to adding new insights to a rich subject, but to using material culture to explore America's relationship with the land of Israel in innovative ways.

Our two guest curators worked closely with the Museum's exhibitions curator, Dr. Karen Mittelman, and collections curator, Dr. Stephen Frank. Mittelman, who served as project director, as always applied her consummate organizational skills and commitment to the highest standards in the field. Frank not only worked with the items in the Museum's collection and supervised all loans to the exhibit, he acted as project director during Dr. Mittelman's maternity leave. The curators were guided through the collections of the Center for Judaic Studies by its librarian, Aviva Astrinsky, and her fine staff. We thank them all for ensuring that this project would be a success.

Thanks are due as well to numerous other Museum and Library staff and consultants, who are named in the acknowledgments.

Financial support came from many sources. The significant and early leadership gift of Constance and Joseph Smukler enabled the project to move forward. Jack Wolgin's major gift was of substantial assistance as well. Israel 50: a partnership among the City of Philadelphia, the Israeli Consulate and Jewish Federation of Greater Philadelphia, and The Walter J. Miller Foundation, provided generous support. The publication of this catalogue was made possible in part by the Lucius N. Littauer Foundation. We would also like to acknowledge the contributions of Richard Abrams, Alma and Sylvan Cohen, the Connelly Foundation, Jeanette and Joe Neubauer, the Samuel S. Fels Fund, Dalck Feith, Laurie Wagman and Irvin Borowsky, Murray H. Shusterman and Fran and Sylvan Tobin.

The Museum gratefully acknowledges The Pew Charitable Trusts for support of exhibitions and programs. Additional arrangements for funding were still being made while the catalogue was being printed; we would like to express our gratitude to the several donors who have made recent commitments to the project, even though we cannot thank them individually.

We would also like to take this opportunity to thank the Boards of the Museum, the Center for Judaic Studies, and the University of Pennsylvania Library. The support, encouragement and enthusiasm of all three were critical to the success of this project.

Margo Bloom, Director
National Museum of American Jewish History

David Ruderman, Director
Center for Judaic Studies
of the University of Pennsylvania

Michael Ryan, Director
Special Collections
University of Pennsylvania Library

Acknowledgments

Our journey to create an exhibition about the American relationship with the Holy Land began in the basement of the University of Pennsylvania's Center for Judaic Studies. Sifting through the Center's archives, we discovered richly detailed landscape drawings and archaeological objects as well as souvenir items, tourist maps, and a commercial series of lantern slides with images of Palestine. The research trail that we followed in the next year convinced us of the pervasiveness, diversity, and far-reaching power of American encounters with the Holy Land. Our search led us to libraries and archival institutions as well as to private collectors and individuals who shared with us a multitude of Holy Land items. This exhibition has been a collaborative effort, and it is a pleasure for us to acknowledge the many individuals and institutions who helped to make this project a reality.

The directors of the three sponsoring institutions have offered unwavering enthusiasm for the project. This exhibition would not have been possible without the persistent efforts of David Ruderman of the Center for Judaic Studies, Margo Bloom of the National Museum of American Jewish History, and Michael Ryan of the University of Pennsylvania Library. We thank them for their support of our work and commitment to bringing this exhibition to fruition.

The staffs of the three institutions have been equally giving of their time and energy. Karen Mittelman, Exhibitions Curator at the National Museum of American Jewish History, guided the project from its inception, encouraging us as we collected material and shaped our ideas. Stephen Frank, the Museum's Collections Curator, arranged loans from a multitude of institutions and his attention to detail kept the project moving smoothly. Jay Nachman, the Museum's Public Relations Manager, helped to copyedit the catalogue and publicize the exhibition. We also benefited from the dedicated support of the staff of the Center for Judaic Studies. Special thanks go to Etty Lassman, who provided invaluable assistance in preparing a computerized inventory of the hundreds of items collected for this project, and to Sheila Allen for her administrative support. We are indebted to librarians Aviva Astrinsky, Judith Leifer, and Pnina Bar-Kana for helping us search the Center's wealth of holdings and for arranging interlibrary loans. Thanks also to Associate Director David Goldenberg, who located valuable material in the Center's archives, and to Sol Cohen, who lent his expertise to the project. We are especially grateful for the creative vision of two individuals—Steven Tucker, the designer of the exhibition at the National Museum of American Jewish History, and Gregory Bear, the designer of this catalogue and of the installation at Van Pelt Library. Their talent and imagination brought to life the exhibition's objects and ideas.

Some of our most enjoyable moments in preparing the exhibition came in our visits to various archives. We were fortunate to work with archivists who shared our enthusiasm for the project and generously opened their collections to us. We particularly appreciate the kind efforts of James Armstrong, Assistant Curator of Collections at the Harvard University Semitic Museum, who let us roam through the Museum's extensive holdings. Jeffrey Spurr of the Harvard University Fine Arts Library gave us access to valuable collections and András Riedlmayer graciously offered his time to guide us through the material. At the University of Pennsylvania, we benefited from the assistance of Bruce Routledge of the University Museum, who helped us gather archaeological artifacts for the exhibition. The University Museum's archivist, Douglas Haller, lent his support to the project, and we are especially grateful for the work of reference archivist, Alessandro Pezzati. At the YIVO Institute for Jewish Research, Zachary Baker, Krysia Fisher,

Leo Greenbaum, Fruma Mohrer, Jenny Romaine, and Marek Web greatly facilitated our research. We received timely assistance from June Miller-Spann at the Chautauqua Institution Archives and from Maja Keech at the Library of Congress. Thanks also to Ellen Smith and the staff of the American Jewish Historical Society, to Susan Woodland of Hadassah Archives, to Kevin Proffitt of the American Jewish Archives, and to Claire Schweriner, a volunteer at the Keneseth Israel Archives, for their part in helping to create this exhibition.

We were fortunate to meet several individuals who lent their personal items to the exhibition. We are particularly indebted to Peter H. Schweitzer, who graciously offered to share his rich collection with us; his contributions have greatly enhanced the exhibition. Special thanks to Frédéric Brenner for allowing us to use the photograph that appears on the catalogue cover. We also appreciate the generosity of Ierach and Dalia Daskal, Stanley and Elaine Ferst, Rela Mintz Geffen, Julie Miller, Isaac Pollak, and Bella Lewensohn Schafer. As they shared items from their collections with us, these individuals also recounted personal stories that furthered our understanding of the relationship between Americans and the Holy Land.

We benefited from the capable efforts of our research assistants, Idana Goldberg and Rebecca Kobrin, as well as the work of intern Elizheva Hurvich. Their willingness to tackle challenging questions and search for material made our job easier and brought new items and ideas to our attention.

Our research was enhanced by discussions with colleagues who participated with us in a year-long fellowship devoted to the study of American Jewish and Israeli culture at the Center for Judaic Studies during 1996-1997. We are grateful to all of the fellows for their interest in our project. Finally, we want to express our special appreciation to Barbara Kirshenblatt-Gimblett and Arthur A. Goren for their invaluable insights into the America-Holy Land dynamic as well as for the essays that they prepared for this catalogue.

Jeffrey Shandler and Beth S. Wenger
Guest Curators

"I'm Building a Palace in Palestine" by Richard Howard
Boston: Daly Music Publisher, 1916

National Museum of American Jewish History

"The Site of Paradise": The Holy Land in American Jewish Imagination
by Jeffrey Shandler and Beth S. Wenger

"Heaven is nearer Palestine than New York." — Robert Morris et al., *Bible Witnesses From Bible Lands,* 1874[1]

The Holy Land is one of the world's most richly imagined places. Revered as the site of Biblical history and the focus of messianic expectations, the Land of Israel has always been more than a geographic place; it also functions as a powerful cultural symbol. The notion of "Zion" as the embodiment of spiritual and, at times, political ideals pervades both American and Jewish cultures, informing personal, national, and religious identities.

American encounters with the Holy Land involved traversing great distances of time and space. Journeys to the region, whether actual or vicarious, enabled Americans to revisit the past and envision the future. Although rooted in notions of the sacred, the Holy Land possesses a highly malleable set of meanings. Generations of Americans have approached the Holy Land as a cultural touchpoint, a landmark and a metaphor for measuring their achievements and ideals.

Today, the State of Israel plays a powerful role in shaping how Americans, both Jews and non-Jews, understand the Holy Land. But unique American attachments to the region developed long before the proclamation of Israeli statehood in 1948. During the preceding century, a watershed of new political, intellectual, and technological developments in the West transformed long-held notions about the Middle East and stimulated new ways of imagining and portraying the region's sacred sites and native inhabitants. American encounters with the Holy Land during the century before the creation of Israel shaped expectations for the new state and continue to inform the ways that Americans understand themselves through their relationship with the Holy Land.

For centuries, Jews, Christians and Muslims have conceived the Land of Israel as sacred territory. Medieval Christian cartographers situated Jerusalem at the center of the world, and Jewish prayer traditionally orients worshipers toward the city. Israel is the land of the Bible, the birthplace of Jesus, and the place where the prophet Mohammed ascended to heaven. As the site of sacred events, the Holy Land has long attracted religious pilgrims of all three faiths.

Beginning in the colonial era, Americans forged unique relationships with the Holy Land. The Puritans defined America as "a new Zion" ordained by Biblical prophecy. For African American slaves, the Holy Land, and particularly the story of the Exodus, served as a metaphor for their own struggle for freedom from bondage.[2] The idea of the Holy Land became a central component of American national identity, influencing the language of the Constitution and inspiring the names of hundreds of cities across the continent.[3] When Jews arrived in the United States, bringing their own attachments to Zion, they encountered a culture already linked to this sacred land thousands of miles away.

The term "Holy Land," the designation most commonly used in the United States during the nineteenth century, demonstrates the extent to which the territory was defined as the land of the Bible—frozen in time and removed from history. Western onlookers seldom acknowledged the region's changing political and cultural dynamic. However, the array of names assigned to the region during the nineteenth and early twentieth centuries—the Levant, Syria,

Jeffrey Shandler is a Dorot Teaching Fellow in the Skirball Department of Hebrew and Judaic Studies at New York University. His forthcoming book, *While America Watches: Televising the Holocaust,* will be published by Oxford University Press.

Beth S. Wenger is the Katz Family Chair in American Jewish History and an assistant professor in the History Department at the University of Pennsylvania. Her most recent book, *New York Jews and the Great Depression: Uncertain Promise,* was published by Yale University Press in 1996.

Palestine, Zion, Eretz Yisrael—reflect shifting territorial boundaries and political sovereignties as well as competing notions of the religious and ideological significance of the land.

American ideas about the Holy Land changed dramatically in the mid-nineteenth century. New modes of travel and the invention of photography made a remote land seem closer and its "exotic" cultures seem more accessible. As archaeologists uncovered the grandeur of ancient civilizations in the Middle East, other modern scholars investigated the spiritual and material culture of the Biblical era, often challenging religious teachings and popular beliefs. At the same time, new political and intellectual movements emerged, sometimes envisioning Palestine as a spiritual utopia and other times as a modern developing nation.

During this century of enormous change, American encounters with the Holy Land proliferated. From tourism to political activism, from personal memoirs to large public events, from the creation of religious articles to the mass production of Palestine images, Americans fashioned new connections with the Holy Land. Christians were often at the forefront

Figure 2
Eastern United States

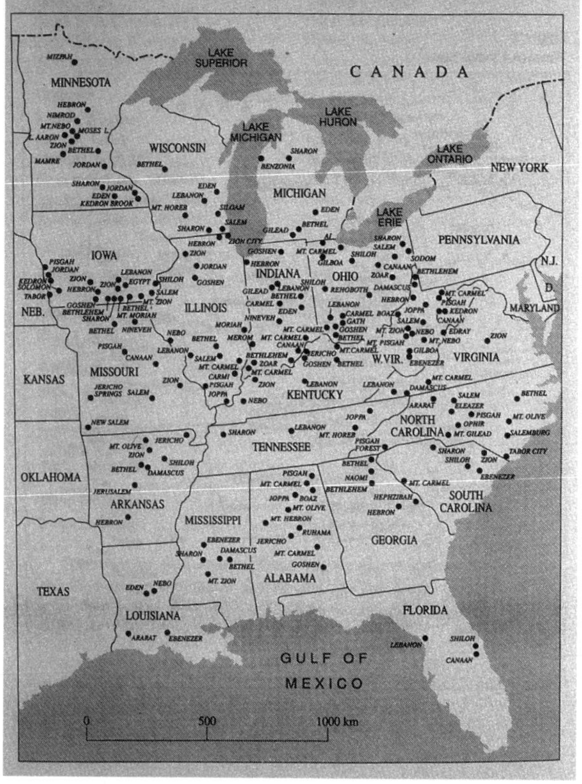

One of a Series of Maps of "Biblical Place-Names in America"
Moshe Davis, *America and the Holy Land: With Eyes Toward Zion-IV.* Copyright 1995 by The International Center for University Teaching of Jewish Civilization. Reproduced with permission of Greenwood Publishing Group, Inc., Westport, CT.

University of Pennsylvania Library

of Holy Land travel, research, and exploration, but the America-Holy Land relationship has also had special implications for American Jews.

The period from the mid-nineteenth to the mid-twentieth century was a turning point in Jewish life, a time when American Jewry emerged as the world's largest Jewish community and developed its own culture, movements and institutions. During this period, the "Land of the Bible" figured as an important site of common interest for Christian and Jewish Americans, despite their divergent interpretations of Scripture. The idea of the Holy Land as a place of shared spiritual heritage was strategically important for Jews as they positioned themselves in American society. American Zionists, for example, often promoted their vision of a Jewish state in Palestine as compatible with, even inspired by, American values of democracy, modernity, and productivity. At the same time, changing images of the Holy Land shaped American Christian perceptions of their Jewish neighbors, both as descendants of ancient Israelites and as a modern community.

Americans have often conceived their

encounters with the Holy Land as ventures into the transcendent, the ancient, the exotic, or the utopian. Yet, in most cases, American excursions to Palestine—whether actual or imagined—began and ended in the United States. These were journeys of self-discovery and national definition in which Americans searched for their own reflections in the mirror of the Holy Land.

Visiting the Holy Land

"With mixed feelings of regret and pleasure I left one spring morning in the year 1909 the shores of New York, on a tour to Palestine, a journey which was to me, as to so many others, a dream of delight . . . Soon we shall stand upon the land of the Patriarchs, Prophets and Kings, walk amid the ruins of fortresses, temples and homes of our glorious ancestors [and] wander through the ancient wonder-fields and cities of the Bible. . . ."

— Benjamin L. Gordon,
New Judea: Jewish Life in Modern Palestine and Egypt, 1919[4]

For centuries, Christian, Muslim, and Jewish pilgrims have journeyed from all over the world to walk in the footsteps of Biblical heroes and worship at the sacred sites of the Holy Land. Following the Civil War, new modes of travel and the advent of a worldwide tourist industry brought a growing number of Americans to Palestine. As travel agencies, cruise lines, and professional guide services multiplied, visiting Palestine was transformed from an individual venture to a large-scale tourist enterprise. The nature of the trips themselves changed, combining traditional elements of religious pilgrimage with features of modern leisure travel. At the same time, the proliferation of Holy Land travel literature and photographs created a parallel industry of "armchair tourism." By the opening decades of the twentieth century, travel to Palestine, whether through actual visits or vicarious tourism, emerged as a centerpiece of American culture and popular imagination.

American travelers brought a variety of expectations to the Holy Land and derived different meanings from their experiences. Depending on the perspective of the traveler, a trip to Palestine could be a religious pilgrimage, an excursion to the exotic Orient, a journey back to the ancient land of the Bible, or a glimpse of the Zionist future. As they toured the Holy Land, Americans mapped their own identities, ideologies, and beliefs onto the region.

The advent of steamships, railways, and later, airplanes, made travel to the Middle East faster, safer, and more comfortable. Although wealthier Americans were the most likely to journey to Palestine, nineteenth-century innovations in steamship technology created a competitive travel industry and drove prices down. As incomes rose in the United States in the post-Civil War years, a growing number of Americans could afford a trip to Palestine.[5] Travel agencies and cruise operators, eager to capitalize on the new enthusiasm for tourism, regularly advertised in American newspapers. In 1926, for example, the Holland-America cruise line offered Palestine tourists a two-month "pleasure cruise exceeding every expectation," complete with gourmet food and entertainment, for a cost of nine hundred dollars.[6] Other companies promoted trips to Palestine as part of a "Grand Tour" with stops throughout Europe and around the Mediterranean.

Holy Land tourism became a burgeoning business in Palestine as well, growing and changing

A Visit to Palestine is the ambition of every true Jew—to set foot on the Holy Land of his ancestors—to see the revival of the glories of ancient Jerusalem, the center of the new Jewish Homeland. ¶ See the progress it made in a decade, to which American Jewry has so liberally contributed.

The Site of the Temple—
JERUSALEM
(מקום המקדש)

An exceptional opportunity to do so, is by booking on the world's fastest passenger ship, the

MAURETANIA

leaving New York February 16, 1929

making short stops at important Mediterranean Tourist Ports. ¶ As usual, there will be special facilities to passengers of Jewish religion for prayers, Kosher kitchen and other matters appreciated by them.

Make your reservations at once. For information apply to

CUNARD LINE

25 BROADWAY   NEW YORK

or to

PALESTINE & ORIENTAL TOURS

122 FIFTH AVENUE   NEW YORK

E. ROSEN, *President*

Regular Fast Freight Service to Jaffa and Haifa

Advertisement for Mauretania, Cunard Line
The New Palestine, 4-11 January 1929

Center for Judaic Studies, University of Pennsylvania Library

with the development of technology and industry. In the 1870s, as *Cook's Tourists' Handbook* explained, most Palestine tourists "pass through the land in the saddle and by night sleep in the tent."[7] Many nineteenth-century visitors considered the "primitive" conditions of Palestine travel an adventure that enhanced the sense of being transported "back in time" to the Biblical era. Local guides or "dragomen" eased the hazards of travel, directing tourists through the unfamiliar and largely undeveloped territory.[8] Published guidebooks advised visitors about how to handle desert conditions, suggesting the best clothing,

food options, and provisions for travel. One author recommended that travelers take condensed milk, noting that the camel's milk provided by Bedouins "generally disagrees with Europeans." He also encouraged visitors to bring an ample supply of "spirit" and plenty of good tobacco to give as gifts to Bedouin guides.[9]

Travel conditions and accommodations improved considerably by the start of the twentieth century. Beginning in 1892, a new Palestine railroad carried visitors from the Jaffa port to Jerusalem, where modern hotels and restaurants catered to their needs.

Jerusalem's King David Hotel, completed in the 1930s, offered tourists not only hot and cold running water, but also the luxuries of an orchestra and chauffeur service.[10] Many tourists came to Palestine to experience the health benefits of the Dead Sea or to vacation on the shores of Tel Aviv, promoted as "the Palestinian 'Atlantic City.'"[11] The "modern traveller is whirled through the country at thirty miles an hour in a motor car," noted one 1920s travel guide, describing the many new options available to Holy Land tourists.[12] Such technological innovations intensified the contrast between ancient and modern Palestine in the eyes of visitors.

Tourists generally came to Palestine with prearranged itineraries. Typically, travelers visited sacred landmarks in and around the walls of Jerusalem, rode through the desert on donkeys or camels, and sampled the foods and merchandise of

Jaffa Gate, Jerusalem
One of hundreds of photographs of the Holy Land produced in the late nineteenth century by the Bonfils Studio, commercial photographers based in Palestine. This image testifies to the various accomodations then available for the Holy Land tourist at the entrance to Jerusalem's Old City, including restaurants, hotels, souvenir shops, tour guides, and porters.

University of Pennsylvania Museum

THE AUTHOR TRAMPING THROUGH PALESTINE

"The Author Tramping Through Palestine"
Milton Goell. *Tramping Through Palestine: Impressions of an American Student in Israeland,* New York: Kensington Press, 1926.

Center for Judaic Studies,
University of Pennsylvania Library

"From New York to Rehoboth and Back"
Yehoash (Solomon Bloomgarten), *Fun Nyu-york biz Rekhovos un tsurik,* New York: Hebrew Publishing Co., 1917. This Yiddish-language travelogue, written by the renowned poet and translator Yehoash, was translated into English as *The Feet of the Messenger.*

Center for Judaic Studies,
University of Pennsylvania Library

"Looking East from Joppa Gate, Jerusalem."
Philadelphia: C.H. Graves, 1903
The text on the reverse of this stereopticon begins: "The greatest charm of Jerusalem is naturally in its historical and religious associations, but its present day aspect and the scenes which are daily enacted in its streets have also the fascination of the unfamiliar."

YIVO Institute for Jewish Research

local markets. At the same time, tourist destinations, routes, and activities varied according to the interests and beliefs of travelers. Published guidebooks led Jews, Christians, and Moslems to their respective holy sites. While Jewish visitors stood "upon the land of the patriarchs," Christian travelers often came to the Holy Land "to follow . . . in the very footsteps of Jesus of Nazareth."[13] Tourists who followed the Zionist Information Bureau's itinerary visited both Jewish settlements and Biblical landmarks, following a route that juxtaposed the holy sites of ancient Israel with the growth of agriculture and industry in the *yishuv*, the Jewish settlement in Palestine.[14]

Actual conditions in Palestine often clashed with American tourists' expectations. Many arrived expecting to see the exalted sites of ancient Israel and expressed shock at the desolate conditions in modern Palestine. "Most travellers have a feeling of disappointment on first seeing Jerusalem," *Cook's Tourists' Handbook* warned prospective visitors, "its magnitude is so much less than the imagination had pictured."[15] Samuel Clemens, later known as Mark Twain, wrote disparagingly in the late 1860s of the inflated descriptions of Palestine that were already common in travel literature. "All these books of travel manage, somehow, to leave us with a sort of vague notion that Palestine was very beautiful," Clemens complained, discovering during his trip that the Holy Land "was a howling wilderness instead of a garden."[16]

However, other visitors found meaning and inspiration in the austerity of Palestine. One nineteenth-century Christian traveler confessed disappointment with the landscape, but found the "habits and customs of the people" to conform with

Photograph of souvenir booth, Jerusalem
The crafts produced by the Bezalel School of Arts and Crafts in Jerusalem proved so popular with tourists that imitations were offered for sale by competing merchants.

YIVO Institute for Jewish Research

Brochure for Vester and Co., the American Colony Stores
The wide array of items advertised for sale include: mother of pearl articles; rosaries; Oriental carpets; the "well known American Colony photographs, lantern slides and cinema films"; hand-painted Jerusalem ceramics; Bibles and prayerbooks in olivewood bindings, as well as "Antiques and Museum Specialties."

Fine Arts Library, Harvard College Library

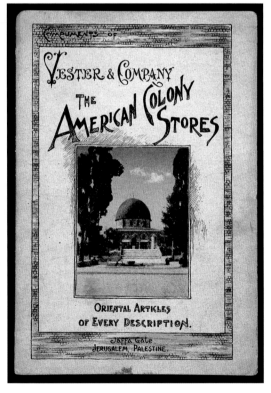

Biblical accounts, proving to her the truthfulness of Scripture.[17] For Zionist travelers, the decline of the region provided justification for Zionist efforts to revivify the land, as tourists observed both "the progress of the Jewish National Home" and the work that remained to be done.[18]

Jews not only observed the Holy Land from a distinct perspective; they were also noteworthy among those being observed by visitors. Many travelers viewed the region's contemporary inhabitants as vestiges of the Biblical era, recasting encounters with Palestinian natives to fit the agenda of their visits. As one of Palestine's indigenous peoples—a diverse population that also included Christian and Muslim Arabs, Bedouins and Samaritans—Jews were often an object of tourist fascination. One Christian traveler, for example, described how "fitting" it was to have a young Jewish woman as his Jerusalem guide, for he "could almost imagine that she was Mary or Martha." The desire to see ancient Israel's past embodied in present-day Palestine was powerful; it shaped the experiences of both Christian and Jewish visitors and recurred repeatedly in American efforts to represent and study the Holy Land.[19]

American travelers materialized their encounters with the Holy Land with an extensive assortment of souvenirs. Ritual, decorative, and edible objects from Palestine enabled American visitors to "bring home" part of the Holy Land. By the turn of the century, merchants offered tourists a wide selection of postcards, depicting holy sites, Biblical settings, street scenes, and regional landscapes. These postcards, sent home by visitors and available for purchase in sets, disseminated images of the Holy Land throughout the United States. Tourists also bought jewelry, ritual items, and trinkets made in Palestine, acquiring material reminders of the Holy Land's ethnic and religious cultures. Souvenirs made of olivewood, stone from the Dead Sea, or sea shells from the Mediterranean coast enabled travelers to

carry away pieces of the Biblical environment. By bringing home Jaffa oranges or Shemen Olive Oil products (advertised as "The World Known Brand from the Holy Land"), American visitors celebrated the natural richness and fertility of the region.[20] Some Jewish tourists purchased items from the Bezalel School of Arts and Crafts, founded in 1906 as a center for creating artistic culture in the *yishuv*. Bezalel carpets, paintings, ceramics, woodwork and metalwork became emblems of the new Zionist culture proudly displayed in American Jewish homes. Objects from the Holy Land also manifested the special sanctity attached to the land itself. While Christian travelers might bring back bottles of water from the Jordan River, religious Jews often returned home with bags of Holy Land soil, designed for use in Jewish burial, as a way of preparing for the messianic age of restoration in the Land of Israel.

Just as material objects made Palestine seem more accessible and tangible, so too, the accounts of famous visitors to the region brought the Holy Land closer to the American public. In the late-nineteenth and early-twentieth centuries, many prominent American figures traveled to Palestine. Herman Melville, Mark Twain, and Joseph Taylor were only a few of the leading authors to publish their impressions of the Holy Land. In the following years, several former and future American presidents as well as a host of scholars and literary figures visited Palestine. Their well-publicized trips furthered American understanding of the region and heightened interest in the Holy Land.[22]

For American Jews, trips to the Holy Land by prominent members of their community held special meaning. The Jewish press closely covered the Palestine visits of Louis Brandeis and Henrietta Szold, using their excursions to trace the progress of the Zionist movement. Other American Jewish philanthropists, activists, scholars, and journalists who journeyed to Palestine reported on the Zionist cause and gave public expression to the connection between American Jews and the Holy Land. For example, Abraham Cahan, editor of the socialist *Jewish Daily Forward*, traveled to Palestine in 1925 and offered his Yiddish-speaking readership a detailed portrait of Jewish life in the region. Cahan's reports from Palestine sold record numbers of newspapers. When, upon his return to New York, he told a large crowd at the Manhattan Opera House that "Palestine is part of my heart," he enhanced American Jewish identification with Palestine and encouraged support for the nascent Zionist movement.[23]

For the many Americans who could not travel to Palestine, literature provided vicarious journeys to the Holy Land. During the century before Israeli statehood, hundreds of Palestine travelogues were published in the United States. Christian travelers produced most of the early accounts, joined in later years by Jewish authors writing in English and Yiddish. Besides providing readers with detailed descriptions of holy sites and monuments, travelogues offered their author's interpretations of the significance of Holy Land travel. Often these linked personal concerns and self-transformation with religious or nationalist issues. Edmond Fleg's 1933 description of his visit to *The Land of Promise,* for example, begins with a foreword to his "unborn grandson" explaining that his travelogue recounts "a voyage to the land of your ancestors, a voyage also within myself, which I would have you make with me."[24]

Photographs, lantern slides, and stereopticons brought Americans their most vivid virtual encounters with the Holy Land. The stereoscope has been described as the nineteenth century's equivalent of television. The three-dimensional effect of stereographs provided the viewer with an unrivaled sense of actually being on the scene.[25] Over five million stereographic images were produced in the United States by the turn of the century, and the Holy Land was among the most popular subjects.[26] Sets of stereoscope slides produced by commercial companies, such as Underwood and Underwood's *Traveling in the Holy Land Through the Stereoscope,* provided views of the Holy Land arranged in a sequence that simulated actual tours of Palestine.[27] The texts accompanying the images explained the history of sites and landscapes, sometimes linking them to Biblical passages.

Lantern slides also sold widely in the United States, often for use as teaching tools in public lectures and Sunday schools. The American Colony in Jerusalem, founded in 1881 as a Christian utopian settlement, joined with Jerusalem entrepreneur Frederick Vester to market photographs and lantern slides. Vester and Company's American Colony Stores, with branches in Jerusalem and New York, sold a variety of Palestine souvenirs, including a popular series of Holy Land images.[28] Photographic studios based in Palestine, like those operated by the Bonfils family, also helped to create a shared visual portrait of the Holy Land. The Bonfils studio was particularly prolific, and its representations of Palestine scenes and ethnic "types" not only sold successfully to American consumers, but also reappeared frequently in book illustrations, becoming standard images of the Holy Land.[29]

Through these photographs, as well as Palestine souvenirs and travelogues, Americans received a popular canon of Holy Land images. Many of these images continue to inform American ideas about the Holy Land.

Representing the Holy Land

I'm building a palace in Palestine,
A beautiful palace for you
(Just for you, you know I love you true).
Where we can live when we grow old,
Where we can love till the desert sands grow cold.
There in a garden of roses, I will be faithful and true.
That's why I'm building sweet Alice a beautiful palace
In Palestine, sweet gal o' mine, for you.
— Richard Howard,
"I'm Building a Palace in Palestine," 1916[30]

Representations of the Holy Land have long been an integral part of Western religious traditions. Both Christians and Jews have produced countless visual images and performances of Biblical landscapes, holy sites, and pivotal moments in sacred history. For centuries these representations have appeared in artwork decorating churches and synagogues, in religious rituals, and in manuscript and book illustrations.

In the modern age new forms of representing the Holy Land flourished. Emerging technologies, such as photography and film, altered the ways that Americans portrayed the Holy Land, as did the West's growing interests in the Middle East. The mass-production of Holy Land images enabled scholars, artists, political activists, and religious leaders to offer diverse visions of the region to vast American audiences.

Representations of ancient Israel allowed viewers to observe—and, presumably, to understand—a remote time and place that had left little record of its physical appearance. The dearth of images from the past, and the apparent austerity of Palestine as Westerners encountered it, created an especially open site, onto which visitors from Europe and America projected their own visions. They portrayed contemporary Palestine sometimes as a living embodiment of the ancient past, other times as the fallen remnant of a once-great culture. Zionists depicted the land as the site of a modernist utopia in the making. All of these visions of the Holy Land

had important implications for American Jews, shaping both their sense of self and their image in the eyes of Christian neighbors.

Before the twentieth century, representations of the Holy Land focused almost exclusively on its ancient past. Even photographs taken of contemporary Palestine were presented as "picturesque" gateways to the Bible.[31] Scholarly efforts to portray ancient Israel concentrated on the city of Jerusalem, especially the Temples of Solomon (ca. 966 - 586 BCE) and Herod (ca. 519 BCE - 70 CE). During the nineteenth century, two- and three-dimensional re-creations of the Temples and their environs emerged as popular tools of public education throughout Europe and the United States, used to help contemporary viewers imagine how these sites might once have appeared. Large-scale panoramic paintings of Holy Land vistas, especially views of Jerusalem, attempted to simulate the pilgrim's experience, so that spectators might feel that they had "actually 'stood within her gates.'"[32]

Scale models, in contrast, provided viewers with

a commanding, omniscient view of sacred sites remote in time and space. One of the most famous models of the Temple Mount, designed by scholar and architect Conrad Schick in 1885, had interchangeable parts that lecturers used to demonstrate the site's changing appearance from ancient times to the nineteenth century, enabling spectators to traverse the millennia in a matter of minutes.[33] Palestine Park, built by the Chautauqua Assembly in 1874, was a particularly ambitious scale model that recreated the landscape of the Holy Land—its mountains, rivers, seas—on a one-quarter-acre site in upstate New York.

Models and panoramas portrayed Jerusalem as an idealized, pious civilization at the height of its splendor. At the same time, the varied designs of these recreations demonstrate the extent to which different artistic and ideological sensibilities shaped visions of the past. For example, a 1913 rendering of King Solomon's Temple by the architectural firm of Helme and Corbett reflects the influence of modern skyscraper design; Harvey Corbett would later design New York City's Rockefeller Center. (See illustration on page 73.)

When archaeology emerged as a popular subject

Model of Old City of Jerusalem
Little is known about this elaborate model, which is believed to have been made by
Moses Kernoosh of Ann Arbor, Michigan in the late nineteenth century.

American Jewish Historical Society, Waltham, Mass., and New York, N.Y.

"Down the Steps of History at Biblical Beth-Shan"
Philadelphia, ca. 1933

University of Pennsylvania Museum

and community leaders, these public presentations of the Israelite past were also a strategic means of legitimating modern Jewish culture by providing it with a distinguished historical pedigree.

This was central to the agenda of the Harvard University Semitic Museum, which opened in 1903 thanks in large measure to the efforts of American Jewish philanthropist Jacob Schiff. The Museum championed Semites as "among the earliest peoples to rise to the state of civilized life," whose contributions to humankind are "so vital and pervasive . . . that, without a knowledge of their source, a large part of modern civilization is unintelligible."[34] Yet the Museum's portrayal of "Semitic" heritage drew on a wide range of sources. Its original installations mixed archaeological artifacts with contemporary ethnographic materials—pottery, clothing, tools, and the like, purchased from Bedouins, Arabs, and Jews living in Palestine at the turn of the century.[35] In addition to ignoring the region's cultural diversity, the Museum's displays implied that, like the rest of the Orient, the Holy Land had remained frozen in time since antiquity. The folkways of its indigenous peoples were presented to museum-goers as vestiges of the life led by Biblical patriarchs millennia earlier. Scholars later renounced this practice, and the modern items were removed from the Semitic Museum's archaeological displays. Yet the notion of Palestine's indigenous populations as primitive compared to the modern Western world has had

during the nineteenth and early twentieth centuries, museums became important sites for presenting the material culture of ancient Israel. Museum exhibitions offered a vision of the Holy Land very different from the idealized presentation of scale models. By displaying early Israelite artifacts alongside those of other ancient Near Eastern civilizations, museums helped situate the Biblical era in a culturally diverse and historically dynamic context. For Jewish scholars lingering implications for their treatment both before and after the establishment of the State of Israel.

The University of Pennsylvania Museum, which opened in 1895, was another major American repository of artifacts and scholarship related to the ancient Near East. The Museum's most important archaeological expedition in Palestine was at Beth-Shan (also known as Beisan), located twelve miles south of the Sea of Galilee. University archaeologists worked at the site periodically from 1921 to 1933, uncovering a wealth of evidence that testifies to the complex intersection of the region's cultures from the Bronze Age through the time of the Crusades. Beginning in 1933, the Museum made Beth-Shan the focus of efforts to foster greater interest in archaeology by inviting the public to walk "down the steps of history" and join the Beth-Shan Society. Membership benefits included monthly reports on the progress of excavations, assistance in planning trips to Palestine, and "authentic reproductions of

Dream of My People
Palestine, 1934
This unusual travelogue features Cantor Yossele Rosenblatt singing sacred melodies and folk songs at Jewish landmarks in Palestine.

Center for Judaic Studies, University of Pennsylvania Library original objects from among the outstanding finds of the season."[36]

As museums were building an American audience for archaeology, world's fairs and international expositions provided another, even more popular stage for presenting Palestine to the public. Representations of the Holy Land at world's fairs combined elements of education, entertainment, and vicarious tourism. At each event, Jewish organizers pursued different strategies for presenting Jews among the nations of the world. At the turn of the century, expositions typically promoted the Holy Land as a locus of the ancient and exotic. By the 1930s, American world's fairs became an important venue for showcasing Zionist visions of a modern Jewish state in Palestine. (See the essay by Barbara Kirshenblatt-Gimblett in this catalogue.)

The Holy Land also came alive for Americans on the stage, concert hall and movie screen. Beginning at the turn of the century, the Holy Land became an occasional topic of American plays, musicals, films, pageants, concerts, dance recitals, and even opera. The creators of these performances used acting, choreography, and melody to convey their sense of the Holy Land's emotional power—whether it was the enduring spirituality of ancient faiths or the promise of creating a new Jewish homeland. Love songs such as "I'm Building a Palace in Palestine" or "A Home in Palestine" from the 1925 Yiddish operetta *A khasene in Palestina* (A Wedding in Palestine) linked theatrical conventions of romantic love with Zionist ardor for the building of a Jewish state.[37] Performances by folksingers and dancers from the *yishuv* demonstrated the new "Palestinian" aesthetic created by Zionists. As dancers Corinne Chochem and Muriel Roth proclaimed, "To see Palestine dance is to see a people reborn."[38] Zionist performances in America culminated in the 1930s and '40s with the production of massive pageants, featuring hundreds, sometimes thousands of participants, which portrayed the Jew's enduring

attachment to the land of Israel. These productions—*Romance of a People* (1933), *The Eternal Road* (1937), *A Flag is Born* (1943), *We Will Never Die* (1946)—were powerful works of propaganda, calling American attention to the perils of anti-Semitism in Europe and exhorting support for the Zionist cause.[39]

Motion pictures have provided some of the most vivid representations of the Holy Land. The earliest American-made films of Palestine were "shorts," lasting little more than one minute, produced by Thomas Edison in 1903. Such titles as "Tourists Embarking at Jaffa," "Jerusalem's Busiest Street," and "Arabian Jewish Dances" offered Americans brief, vicarious excursions to the "exotic" Middle East via the nickelodeon. Other early works of American cinema—including D. W. Griffith's *Judith of Bethulia* (1914) and *Intolerance* (1916), or Cecil B. DeMille's first, silent version of the *Ten Commandments* (1923)—imaginatively reenacted epic moments from Biblical times.

Political Zionism "was born at almost exactly the same time as cinema," and the novelty of filmed presentations of the *yishuv* underscored the impact of their message.[40] During the 1920s and '30s, Zionist organizations made regular use of the cinema to disseminate propaganda and solicit support from Americans with such films as *Rebirth of a Nation* (1926) and *Land of Promise* (1935). At the same time, Christian educators turned to film as an innovative way to familiarize students with the sites of the Middle East. In 1930, Reverend Albert C. Saxman of Latrobe, Pennsylvania, promoted his travelogue *Palestine As We See It Today* by declaring that the film would provide church workers with "an evening that will revitalize their entire religious life, and give them a wealth of material that they can draw from for years to come."[41] The full sweep of Palestine's history is traced in *The Holy Land from Abraham to Allenby*, a British-made film released in the United States in 1941 by the Harmon Foundation, an organization dedicated to promoting progressive Christian

Three-dimensional Rosh Hashanah card
Germany, ca. 1910
Many greeting cards for the Jewish new year featured Zionist images, from views of Palestine to the portraits of the movement's leaders. Sending these cards to family and friends was one of various ways of incorporating a commitment to Zionism into the traditional Jewish holiday calendar.

National Museum of American Jewish History

of engaging their pupils. Teaching Jewish children modern Hebrew folksongs and "Palestinian" dances offered them a physical, emotional and communal experience of Zionism.[42] Staging Bible plays at a Sunday school or simulating kibbutz life at a summer camp encouraged American youngsters to imagine themselves as part of the Israelite past or the Zionist future.

Perhaps the most frequent and intimate American encounters with the Holy Land took place in family homes. Ritual and decorative objects from Palestine domesticated the exotic and spiritually-charged Holy Land, making it a familiar presence in daily life. The home became the most pervasive venue for establishing an aesthetic of the Holy Land. Certain motifs and images—such as palm trees and scenes of worshippers at the Western Wall—became familiar through reproductions circulated in American consumer culture. In addition to situating the Land of Israel in traditional ritual and organized political activity, the home offered American Jews a place to establish their own private attachments to this distant land. For example, Julie Miller of New York City recalls that a highlight of visiting the Bronx home of her grandmother, Minnie Singer Miller, was drinking milk from a special silver cup made in Palestine and decorated with palm trees and camels. During these visits, Julie's grandmother would give her pennies to place in a blue and white *pushke*, or almsbox.[43]

pedagogy. As in other representations of the Holy Land, the film used footage of daily life among modern Bedouins and Samaritans to represent scenes from the Bible, thereby calling upon the Palestinian present to serve as a point of entry to its past.

Americans were not only audiences for enactments of the Holy Land; in religious schools and summer camps they became performers as well. In the early decades of the twentieth century, religious educators in the United States began to emphasize the importance of crafts and performing arts as means

Studying the Holy Land

"At no period during many past centuries has greater interest been felt in the cities of the East, especially of Jerusalem, than at present, when as is believed, the secrets hidden beneath its soil for near upon 2,000 years are about to be disclosed...." — *New York Times,* April 2, 1871[44]

Modern scholarship revolutionized the way that Americans conceptualized the Holy Land. Beginning in the mid-nineteenth century, archaeologists, geologists, artists, photographers and ethnographers traveled to the Middle East to excavate the physical remains, paint the landscapes, explore the geography, and document the natural history and populations. The works of writers, scholars, and artists contributed to the American "rediscovery" of the Holy Land and helped to make the ancient world a central American preoccupation.

Those who studied the Holy Land pursued diverse, sometimes conflicting, agendas. Despite the language and methodology of secular research, Holy Land scholarship was inextricably intertwined with religious and political interests. Many professional and amateur scholars sought to prove the veracity of Biblical texts and were often torn between the imperatives of their faith and a commitment to "science." Other scholars, interested in discovering clues to the rise and fall of the grand civilizations of the ancient Middle East, portrayed the region's contemporary inhabitants as exotic primitives, evidence of the decline of the Orient. American Christians and Jews brought different ideologies and missions to the study of the Holy Land, but their shared interest in the region and its history fostered ties between the two communities.

As the Middle East became more accessible to Western visitors in the nineteenth century, seeing the Holy Land became a fundamental component of its understanding. Before the popularization of photography, landscape art was the dominant form of depicting the Holy Land and other remote locations. Although many nineteenth-century landscapes of the region were produced by European artists, their works were widely exhibited to American audiences and sold in reproductions. These richly detailed panoramic canvases and prints simulated the vistas, holy sites and inhabitants of the Middle East, often suggesting that the scenes remained unchanged from ancient to modern times. David Roberts' Holy Land drawings, widely circulated and reprinted since their first publication in 1842, were described in Reverend George Croly's accompanying narrative as enabling the spectator to feel that "he is traversing the very ground" where Biblical figures had walked and that "he stands where they taught, suffered, and triumphed."[45]

Artistic renderings of the Holy Land were more than decorative and inspirational items, they were also tools of scholarship. Sketch artists often accompanied Holy Land researchers, who depended upon visual inventories of sites, artifacts, and topography for their investigations. Nineteenth-century artistic compositions of the Holy Land also influenced the first photographers who visited the Middle East in the 1840s. Even after the late nineteenth century, when photographs of the region were widely produced and circulated, landscape art continued to shape American perceptions of the Holy Land.[46]

Because the Holy Land was considered sacred terrain, its geography, flora and fauna held special interest for secular and religious scholars. Researchers from Europe and the United States employed the

"Mount of Olives From City Wall"
American Colony Photographers, Vester & Co. Jerusalem, ca. 1900
This turn-of-the-century lantern slide is specially tinted in vibrant hues,
giving viewers a heightened sense of Palestine's landscape.

Center for Judaic Studies, University of Pennsylvania Library

scientific practice of taxonomy, perfected in the nineteenth century, to inventory the physical environment of modern Palestine and index it to the region's sacred, ancient past. The first Holy Land scholars were devout Christians who turned to the sciences to confirm the Bible's veracity and illuminate their understanding of its teachings. Edward Robinson, the pioneer of Holy Land research in America, produced a pathbreaking three-volume study of Palestinian archaeology and geography in 1841.[47] Robinson's efforts to demonstrate the authenticity of the Bible inspired a generation of scholars on both sides of the Atlantic. John Kitto's

1850 *Scripture Lands,* for example, provided readers with an index locating Biblical place names on topographical maps of Palestine, as well as individual chapters on the country's almond and fig trees, goats, bulls, and bears.[48]

The professional enthusiasm for documenting and scrutinizing the natural history of the "Land of the Bible" was shared by amateur groups and individuals. Working on behalf of the America Holy-Land Exploration Society in 1874, Robert Morris offered its members a catalog of Palestine "specimens"—stone, woods, shells, flowers, and other materials—each with scriptural references as

Flowers from the Holy Land
The extensive interest in the natural history of the Holy Land can be seen even in tourist souvenirs. Books of pressed flowers from the Holy Land, bound with olivewood covers, were popular mementos purchased by visitors to Palestine at the turn of the century. Different books were created for Jewish and Christian customers.

prooftexts. The Society sold the specimens throughout the country to individuals, Masonic Lodges, and Sunday schools; a "Holy Land Cabinet" complete with 150 sacred objects could be purchased for only ten dollars.[49] Natural history provided Americans with the ability to see and feel the Holy Land and to use "the works of nature" as "object-lessons" to interpret the Bible.[50]

Holy Land scholarship was most often used in defense of Christian claims, but American Jews also produced studies that supported their religious beliefs and political agendas. Such works became more frequent in the early twentieth century, with the advent of political Zionism. For example, as the British were taking control of Palestine from the Ottoman Empire in 1917, Samuel Isaacs authored *The True Boundaries of the Holy Land,* a volume that called for the "restoration of a national Homeland to the Jews" according to the geographical boundaries described in the Book of Numbers.[51]

The field of archaeology burgeoned like no other

area of Holy Land studies during the late nineteenth and early twentieth centuries, and its discoveries sparked an American fascination with studying the Holy Land. Like other Holy Land scholars, the first archaeologists used their research to authenticate holy scriptures. "The Bible," explained prominent Near East scholar William Albright, "invariably requires archaeological elucidation before it becomes completely intelligible."[52] However, archaeological findings often created dilemmas for scholars, as the pursuit of scientific truth challenged their religious convictions.[53]

Both political and religious interests were embedded in archaeological research. Excavations in Palestine became a source of American pride. Britain's

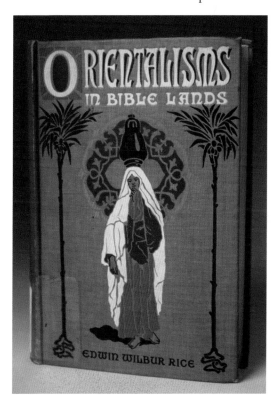

Orientalisms in Bible Lands by Edwin Wilbur Rice
Philadelphia: American Sunday-School Union, 1910

Excavation at Beth-Shan
Palestine, 1926

Palestine Exploration Fund had been a dominant presence in Holy Land excavation in the nineteenth century, and by the 1870s, Americans believed that they, too, should share in the exploration of Bible lands. The American Palestine Exploration Society cooperated with its British counterpart in dividing research territories in the region, but Americans considered it of utmost importance for their nation to stake a claim in uncovering the riches of the Holy Land. At the same time, the emerging fields of archaeology and Semitic studies unsettled the intellectual terrain of America's Protestant-dominated academies, challenging religious authority and

providing the first opportunity for Jews, such as Morris Jastrow and Cyrus Adler, to receive faculty appointments.[54]

Interest in archaeology extended beyond the academy, reaching the general public through museum exhibitions, amateur societies, and popular publications that made the field accessible and adventuresome. Reverend James Baikie, for example, introduced readers of his 1923 book, *The Glamour of Near East Excavation,* to an archaeological "treasure-hunt" for clues to the ancient world.[55] The "true aim of archaeology," he explained, is "to make the life of the dead past live again before the eyes of the present generation."[56]

Studying the Holy Land involved not only excavating Palestine's physical remains, but also scrutinizing its people and cultures. Many professional and amateur scholars conflated ancient and modern Palestine, believing as one American traveler wrote in 1897, that "the people of Palestine have changed less in their manner of living, customs, and their prejudices, than those of any other country; they are almost the same to-day that they were two thousand and more years ago."[57] This perspective exemplifies the "Orientalist" portrayal of Palestine long shared by most Westerners. American observers in the nineteenth and twentieth centuries typically defined Palestine's population as primitive "others," living in exotic and unchanging conditions, whose culture required the perspective of the modern Western scholar to be properly understood.[58]

Ethnographies of Palestine abounded in travel literature, religious geographies, and scholarly research. Captivated by the Oriental aesthetic, Americans offered an inventory of the region's ethnic "types," complete with detailed descriptions of the "Syrian Jewess," the "Bedouin nomad," or the "whirling

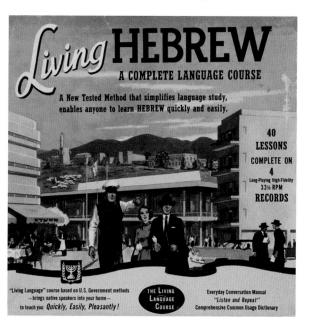

"Living Hebrew"
New York: Living Language Courses, 1958
Following the establishment of the State of Israel, American study of modern Hebrew flourished in classrooms and through self-instruction, as with this set of records.

Collection of Jeffrey Shandler

dervish." Palestine's native inhabitants were variously portrayed as mysterious and romantic or backward and uncivilized. At the same time, Americans viewed Oriental culture as a living conduit to the world of the Bible. The rituals, tools, costume, foodways and music of Palestinian natives were studied as vestiges of ancient Middle Eastern culture. In *Orientalisms in Bible Lands,* published in 1910 by the American Sunday-School Union, Edwin Rice insisted that, "we must transport ourselves into the conditions and spirit of this Oriental life . . . or often miss the divine message of the Bible."[59]

Ethnographic studies frequently reflected the specific cultural concerns of their authors. For example, whereas Christian accounts typically portrayed the contemporary Jewish population in Palestine as impoverished and debased, some Jewish ethnographers sought to refute such claims.[60] Thus, Elkan Adler's 1905 survey of *Jews in Many Lands* argued that the Jewish community of Jerusalem was "much better than its reputation" of indigence and filth.[61]

After the establishment of the *yishuv,* Jewish scholarship of the Holy Land increasingly focused on the study of Zionist ideology and culture. The Zionist commitment to promoting Hebrew as the language of the future Jewish state sparked an American Jewish interest in learning modern Hebrew and supporting its literature and culture. The study of modern Hebrew in the United States was limited in the period before Israeli statehood, but Americans worked to fulfill and perpetuate Israel's "spiritual needs" in the form of modern Hebrew culture, supporting such organizations as the Palestine Hebrew Culture Fund and the Society of Friends of the "Ohel" Hebrew Dramatic Theater. An appeal for support for the latter organization linked the archaeological riches of Palestine with the need to establish a Hebrew national theater: "In no country has a nation more eternity overhead and under its feet than in Palestine.... The historic treasures of the nation, partly buried in literature and folk-lore, are brought to light and life again on the stage to serve as a guide to the people struggling for its renaissance."[62]

Supporting the Holy Land

Dear American Children: Thank you for the money you have put in this bag. It helps the children of Israel become as healthy and happy as the children of America. It brings them good food, good playgrounds and good medical care. — Fundraising bag, Hadassah, ca. 1937[63]

Providing support has long been a mainstay of diaspora relationships with the Holy Land. Followers of all Western faiths have worked to maintain religious communities, houses of worship, and shrines in the region. For the American Jewish community, support for the Holy Land has embraced a wide range of activities—from collecting funds to lobbying politicians, from buying goods made in the *yishuv* to serving in Jewish military units based in Palestine.

Zionism moved to the forefront of American Jewish philanthropy during the twentieth century, but fundraising for Jews in the Holy Land had begun generations before the first groups of Zionist settlers arrived in the late 1800s. Since the colonial era, coreligionists in the United States provided financial support to the small number of pious Jews who had lived in Palestine for centuries. Aid went to the largely impoverished community primarily through donations to its synagogues, rabbinical academies, orphanages, old-age homes, and public kitchens. Appeals to maintain these institutions invoked the traditional Jewish obligation of almsgiving as an act of *tzedakah* (righteousness) and promised donors both spiritual and material rewards in return for their philanthropy. Thus, a 1763 letter requesting a donation, sent from Palestine to Philadelphia's Michael Gratz, concludes, "May God recompense him for his good deeds with many and redoubled good, with prosperity, with joy from children and children's children who are wise and sage, like ripened olives surrounding his table, and in all that he turn shall he be successful."[64]

American Jewish support for the Land of Israel has been shaped by both traditional notions of charity and modern American philanthropic practices. This is particularly apparent in American Jewry's extensive involvement in Zionism. While Zionism was far from popular in early twentieth century America, it soon spawned numerous organizations and activities that reflected the diverse religious and political commitments of American Jews. Zionist leaders established powerful ties between financial and ideological support, epitomized by the creation of the *shekel* in 1897. This symbolic donation, named after the currency of ancient Israel, allowed Americans who contributed fifty cents to the World Zionist Organization to become voting members in Zionist Congress elections.

American Zionists developed a distinct approach to participating in the effort to establish a Jewish state in Palestine. Zionists on the other side of the Atlantic Ocean saw the *yishuv* as a solution to the inherently problematic existence of European Jewry. American Zionists, however, championed the need for a Jewish state abroad while continuing their commitment to maintaining Jewish communities in the United States. Throughout the first half of the twentieth century, American Jews debated whether Zionism was compatible with American patriotism and with Judaism.[65]

Matzoh Fund Stamp
Central Committee Knesseth Israel of Jerusalem, Palestine, n.d.
This pair of fundraising stamps contrasts a middle-class American family at the seder table with indigent Jews in Palestine receiving Passover food donations.

National Museum of American Jewish History

or fighting in the Jewish Legion during World War I. However, most American Zionists did not envision settling in Palestine as their goal. Instead, they realized their ties to the *yishuv* through an array of cultural activities, many of which centered around providing financial support for the new Jewish homeland. These practices not only provided American Zionists with an important symbolic attachment to the Land of Israel but also evolved into an important component of Jewish identity and culture in America. (See the essay by Arthur A. Goren in this catalogue.)

American Jews played a key financial role in establishing the infrastructure of the *yishuv* by helping Zionist organizations purchase land in Palestine and by underwriting banks, schools, hospitals and other essential community institutions. The American-Palestine Bank of Tel Aviv even invited

Only a small number of Jews emigrated from the United States to Palestine during the first four decades of the twentieth century; a few spent extended periods of time helping to build Jewish settlements American Jews to "help build Palestine at a profit to yourself" by becoming shareholders.[66] The amount of money Zionists raised in the United States rose rapidly; the United Palestine Appeal reported an

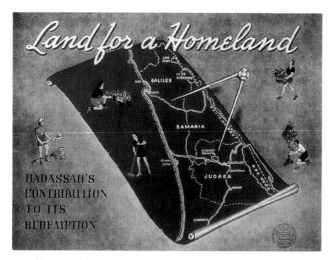

Pamphlet, "Land for a Homeland"
Hadassah, ca. 1940

compelling role models of the "new" Jewish man and woman—proud, athletic, activist, visionary, and committed to modern, collectivist ideals. Yet these were exemplars for American Jews to admire and support, rather than imitate. Zionist propaganda depicted female pioneers in Palestine at work on farms and in factories. In contrast, Zionist women in the United States were exhorted to "serve Palestine with the labor of your hands" and form sewing circles; these produced clothing for the *halutzim* while providing American Jewish women with opportunities to socialize and promote the Zionist cause.[69]

increase from $2,830,000 collected during the years 1914-1918 to $12,748,000 raised in 1922-1926.[67] Beginning in the 1920s, advertisers promoted consumerism as a form of Zionist advocacy, urging the readers of American Zionist periodicals to buy wine, almonds, olive oil, oranges, honey, and other produce from Palestine. Besides supporting the growth of Jewish-owned farms and businesses, consumers could savor the tastes—and even, in the case of Palestine Cigarettes, the aroma—of the Holy Land.

While many *halutzim* (Zionist pioneers) championed the collective life prescribed by socialist principles, American Zionists took pride in owning property in Palestine, and they supported commercial activity and the development of urban culture in the *yishuv*. Indeed, American Zionists often held up their nation's ideals of democracy, consensus building, and economic prosperity as goals for the Jewish state. Even the American landscape sometimes served as a model for visions of the *yishuv*; promotions for new colonies and agricultural enterprises characterized Palestine as "the California of the Orient."[68]

Halutzim provided American Zionists with

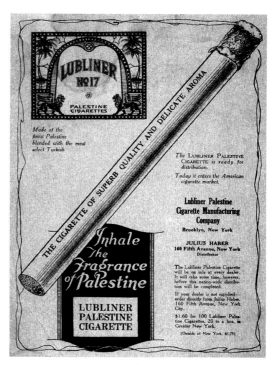

Advertisement for Lubliner Palestine Cigarettes
The New Palestine, 27 March 1925

During the first decades of the twentieth century, American Jews established a plethora of Zionist organizations—political groups, charities, fraternal societies, men's, women's and youth groups, publishers, educational institutions, and summer camps. Some organizations attracted vast memberships; by 1941, over 100,000 women were members of Hadassah, founded by Henrietta Szold in New York City in 1912. Zionism in the United States quickly became a corporate enterprise, with organizations that were modeled, in large measure, on the structure of American clubs, charities and fraternal orders. For example, Bnai Zion, the Fraternal Zionist Organization of America, championed "Americanism, Zionism and Fraternalism" as its "three cardinal principles." In addition to raising funds for the *yishuv* and supporting Hebrew cultural activities in both the United States and Palestine, Bnai Zion promoted "a deep devotion and loyalty to the ideals of American democracy" and provided its members with health care, life insurance and burial grounds.[70]

Through their extensive network of organizations, American Zionists developed a wide range of fundraising activities and invested the act of donating money to support the *yishuv* with great symbolic value. Collecting contributions for the Zionist cause became, in turn, a form of organized outreach to America's expanding Jewish community. Zionist fundraising events emerged as important rituals in American Jewish culture; they helped define community identity and for many inspired national pride.

The Jewish National Fund (Keren Kayemet L'Yisrael), founded in Europe in 1901, played a leading role in establishing fundraising practices that flourished on both sides of the Atlantic. The blue-and-white JNF *pushke*, created in 1904, soon became one of the most widely recognized icons of the Zionist cause. A promotional brochure from the 1940s explained to potential donors that the JNF box "is a mighty instrument for good" and "an eloquent symbol of our people's faith in, and hope for, a better future in a peaceful world." Many American Jews displayed the JNF box as a sign of ethnic solidarity as well as an indication that they had joined "the noble company of the Builders of Zion."[71]

Zionism also inspired American Jews to stage all manner of public events: rallies, demonstrations, parades, pageants, banquets, lectures, dances, concerts, fundraisers, holiday celebrations. Often these were hybrid occasions, combining Jewish rituals with celebrity appearances and featuring musical performances from traditional, Zionist, popular and classical repertoires. Typically, these programs concluded with the singing of both America's national anthem and the Zionist anthem *"Hatikvah."* Public events played a vital role in American Zionist culture. Fusing community spirit with Zionist ideology, they created opportunities for Jews to present themselves to the general American public as a nation with a proud history and a promising future.

Giving contributors some tangible reminder of their support—such as a certificate, badge, pin, trophy, or plaque—became a crucial component of Zionist fundraising. These tokens of appreciation provided American Zionists with measures of their generosity and service and became valued symbols of their status within the hierarchy of Zionist organizations. These items also materialized American Jewish connections to the distant *yishuv*, familiarized the American public with Zionist icons, and served as "badges of honor" that could be displayed on clothing or in homes and businesses.

As was also the case with European Jewry, the images reproduced on Zionist testimonials "construed . . . a national landscape" in the minds of American Jews and "recast traditional Jewish images in a national context."[72] Certificates acknowledging donations to the JNF, Hadassah, and other organizations were frequently adorned with idealized images of muscular *halutzim* working the land. JNF stamps featuring the portraits of the movement's leaders and Zionism's most enduring symbol, the blue and white banner, became powerful emblems of a potential nation, analogous to the official flags and postage of sovereign states. One of the most popular and symbolically powerful acts of support for the *yishuv* from abroad was donating money to plant trees in Palestine, fulfilling the vision of early Zionist leaders to "reforest" the Land of Israel. Recalling the trees that he helped plant in Palestine as a child in England, historian Simon Schama observed, "The trees were our proxy immigrants, the forests our implantation.... To create a Jewish forest was to go back to the beginning of our place in the world, the nursery of the nation."[73]

Epilogue: From Palestine to the State of Israel

In honor of your birthday, a tree has been planted in Israel in your name . . .
Your day to water it is Thursday!
—Birthday card, American Greetings, ca. 1997[74]

The final decade before Israeli statehood witnessed rapid, profound changes in American relationships with Palestine. Since the beginning of the century, American Zionists had championed their cause as a remedy for European anti-Semitism. With the Nazi rise to power in the 1930s and the inauguration of Hitler's campaign to conquer Europe and purge it of Jews, Zionists redoubled their efforts to establish a Jewish state in Palestine as a refuge for European Jewry. Following the end of World War II and the revelation of the Holocaust, many Americans—Jews and non-Jews alike—embraced the notion that the destruction of European Jewish life could be redeemed with the birth of a new Jewish state.

The establishment of the State of Israel on May 14, 1948 inaugurated a new era in American encounters with the Holy Land. As a new democracy in the Middle East, Israel eventually emerged as a strategic ally of the United States in international politics. While the two nations maintain a strong alliance, their relationship has been fraught with tensions, especially with regard to Israel's ongoing conflicts with neighboring Arab states and Palestinians living under its control. The ties between American Jewry and Israel are no less complex. American Jews continue to provide extensive financial and activist support for Zionism; for many, Israel plays a powerful, even central, role in their sense of Jewish identity. Modern Israeli culture has become part of American Jewish life through celebrations of Yom Ha-atzma'ut (Israel Independence Day), translations of contemporary Hebrew literature, recordings of popular Israeli music, and even the consumption of falafel and other Middle Eastern foods. At the same time, Israeli and American Jews are often struck by how different their two cultures have become, despite the ideal vision that Jews share an essential commonality through time and across geographic boundaries.

Even with these many changes over the past fifty years, American encounters with Israel still bear the imprint of the preceding century. Christians, Jews and Muslims still journey from the United States to Israel to visit ancient sacred sites and to savor the "exotic" pleasures of the Middle East. Vicarious travel to Israel has been enhanced by newer technologies, including television, video, and computers, while Israeli history and culture have become the subject of

Playing cards
El Al Airlines, ca. 1970
This promotional item distributed by Israel's national airline replaces traditional face cards with Biblical heroes.
Reproduced by permission, El Al Airlines

Collection of Jeffrey Shandler

popular American fiction, Hollywood dramas and even a Broadway musical. Artifacts of modern Israeli culture, from fine art to kitsch, adorn many American Jewish homes. Through philanthropy, American Zionists continue to support a wide variety of institutions in Israel, and American-Israeli relations figure prominently in Jewish political activism in the United States.

The relationships with the Holy Land that Jewish and non-Jewish Americans have created during the past half-century are not only the result of the establishment of the State of Israel; they also continue to reflect the dynamics of American life in general and American Jewish culture in particular. In the United States, hopes for peace in the Middle East epitomize the desire to see America's values of democracy and tolerance adopted as an international ideal. Even as the land is more accessible to visits, both actual and virtual, Israel continues to serve as an important symbol for American Jews, representing shared cultural aspirations as well as alternatives to the lives that Jews maintain in the diaspora.

In the last fifty years, the Jewish communities of the United States and Israel have become interdependent, relying on one another as comparative points of reference to measure Jewish identity, politics, and culture. As America and Israel emerge as distinct centers of Jewish life in the late twentieth century, the Holy Land remains an even more complicated and multilayered site of American imagination.

Notes

[1] Robert Morris et al., *Bible Witnesses From Bible Lands* (New York: American Holy-Land Exploration, 1874), p. 174.

[2] See Albert J. Raboteau, "African Americans, Exodus, and the American Israel," in David G. Hackett, ed., *Religion and American Culture: A Reader*, (New York: Routledge, 1995), pp. 73-86.

[3] See Moshe Davis, "The Holy Land Idea in American Spiritual History," in Moshe Davis, ed., *With Eyes Toward Zion: Scholars Colloquium on America-Holy Land Studies* (New York: Arno Press, 1977), pp. 3-33. Davis was a pioneer in America-Holy Land studies; his collected volumes, reprints, and bibliographic guides provide a comprehensive overview of both primary source material and scholarly research about America and the Holy Land.

[4] Benjamin L. Gordon, *New Judea: Jewish Life in Modern Palestine and Egypt* (Philadelphia: Julius H. Greenstone, 1919), pp. 1, 25-26.

[5] David Klatzker, "American Christian Travelers to the Holy Land, 1821-1939," in Moshe Davis and Yehoshua Ben-Arieh, eds., *With Eyes Toward Zion III: Western Societies and the Holy Land* (New York: Praeger Publishers, 1991), p. 72 n.3.

[6] Advertisement for Holland-America Line, *New York Times*, 17 January 1926.

[7] *Cook's Tourists' Handbook for Palestine and Syria* (London: Thomas Cook & Son, 1876), p. iii.

[8] Lester I. Vogel, *To See a Promised Land: Americans and the Holy Land in the Nineteenth Century* (University Park: Pennsylvania State University Press, 1993), pp. 61-65.

[9] "A Few Hints to Travellers in the East, Especially the Desert," in Rev. Harry Jones, *Past and Present in the East* (London: Religious Tract Society, 1881), pp. 142-44.

[10] Advertisement for King David Hotel, *Guide to New Palestine,* Ninth Edition (Jerusalem: Benjamin Lewensohn for the Zionist Information Bureau for Tourists in Palestine, 1936-1937), p. 95.

[11] Advertisement for Palestine & Oriental Shipping Service Co., *The New Palestine*, 20 April 1923, p. 294.

[12] Revered Rennie MacInnes, pamphlet, "Notes for Travellers: By Road and Rail in Palestine and Syria," (London: H.B. Skinner and Co., ca. 1920s), Harvard Semitic Museum Collection, Box 126, Fine Arts Library, Harvard University.

[13] Frank Willoughby, pamphlet, "What I Saw In Jerusalem," (New York: Palestine Christian Memorial Association, 1926), p. 13, Harvard Semitic Museum Collection, Box 126, Fine Arts Library, Harvard University.

[14] *Guide to New Palestine*, pp. 100-102.

[15] *Cook's Tourists' Handbook for Palestine and Syria*, p. 112.

[16] Samuel Clemens, *Traveling with the Innocents Abroad*, ed. D. M. McKeithan (Norman: University of Oklahoma Press, 1958), pp. 303-304.

[17] Emily Severance, as cited in Vogel, *To See a Promised Land*, p. 76.

[18] *Guide to New Palestine*, p. 9.

[19] Willoughby, "What I Saw In Jerusalem," p. 6. Fine Arts Library, Harvard University.

[20] Advertisement for Shemen Olive Oil products, *Guide to New Palestine*, p. 4.

[21] Herman Melville, *Clarel: A Poem and Pilgrimmage in the Holy Land*, (1876; reprint, New York: Hendricks House, 1960); Samuel Clemens, *The Innocents Abroad; or, The New Pilgrims' Progress* (Hartford, Conn.: American Publishing Co., 1869); Joseph I. Taylor, *A Gyre Thro' the Orient* (Princeton, N.J.: Republican Print and Job Printing Office, 1869).

[22] Among the many other American authors who traveled to the Holy Land were John Lloyd Stephens, William Cullen Bryant, and John W. De Forest. Presidents Theodore Roosevelt, Ulysses S. Grant, and John F. Kennedy visited Palestine at some point during their lives, and Abraham Lincoln was reported to have been considering a journey to the Holy Land before his assassination. See Lester Vogel, *To See a Promised Land*, pp. 41-93.

[23] Abraham Cahan, as cited in Moses Rischin, "The Promised Land in 1925: America, Palestine, and Abraham Cahan," *YIVO Annual* 22 (1995), p. 98.

[24] Edmond Fleg, *The Land of Promise*, trans. Louise Waterman Wise (New York: Macauley, 1933), p. 21.

[25] Jonathan Crary, *Techniques of the Observer : On Vision and Modernity in the Nineteenth Century* (Cambridge, Mass.: MIT Press, 1990), pp. 122-24.

26 Davis, *The Landscape of Belief: Encountering the Holy Land in Nineteenth Century American Art and Culture* (Princeton: Princeton University Press, 1996), pp. 74-76.

27 Jesse Lyman Hurlbut, *Traveling in the Holy Land Through the Stereoscope* (New York: Underwood & Underwood, 1900).

28 Brochure, "Vester & Company, The American Colony Stores," ca. 1920s, Harvard Semitic Museum Collection, Box 126, Fine Arts Library, Harvard University; see also Eyal Onne, *Photographic Heritage of the Holy Land, 1839-1914* (Manchester, England: Institute of Advanced Studies, Manchester Polytechnic, 1980), p. 15.

29 Onne, *Photographic Heritage of the Holy Land*, pp. 13-14, 90.

30 Sheet music, Richard Howard, "I'm Building a Palace in Palestine" (Boston: Daly Music Publisher, 1916), National Museum of American Jewish History.

31 See Onne, *Photographic Heritage of the Holy Land 1839-1914*, pp. 12-14.

32 Rev. Edward L. Clark, as cited in Israel P. Warren, *Descriptive Book and Key Plates of Selous' Two Grand Pictures of Jerusalem, Ancient and Modern* (Boston: Elliot, Blakeslee and Noyes, 1873), p. B.

33 See Haim Goren and Rehav Rubin, "Conrad Schick's Models of Jerusalem and Its Monuments," *Palestine Exploration Quarterly* 128 (1996), pp. 103-24.

34 Harvard Semitic Museum, "Statement" (reprint from *Harvard Alumni Bulletin*, 28 January 1926), folder: Harvard University Semitic Museum History, Semitic Museum, Harvard University.

35 "Semitic Museum," reprinted from *Harvard University Handbook*, 1902, p. 87, folder: Harvard University Semitic Museum History, Semitic Museum, Harvard University.

36 "Down the Steps of History at Biblical Beth-Shan," brochure, ca. 1933, Beth Shan Society, Box 4, University of Pennsylvania Museum Archives.

37 Howard, "I'm Building A Palace in Palestine"; sheet music, Louis Gilrod and Peretz Sandler, "A Heim in Palestine," (New York: Trio press, 1925), National Museum of American Jewish History.

38 Corinne Chochem and Muriel Roth, *Palestine Dances! Folk Dances of Palestine* (New York: Berman House, 1941), p. 8.

39 See Atay Citron, "Pageantry and Theater in the Service of Jewish Nationalism in the United States, 1933-1946," Ph.D. diss., New York University, 1989.

40 Hillel Tryster, *Israel before Israel: Silent Cinema in the Holy Land* (Jerusalem: Steven Spielberg Jewish Film Archive, 1995), pp. 1, 10.

41 Brochure, "Palestine As We See It Today," ca. 1930, Harvard University Semitic Museum Collection, Box 126, Fine Arts Library, Harvard University.

42 See Jenna Weissman Joselit with Karen S. Mittelman, eds., *A Worthy Use of Summer: Jewish Summer Camping in America* (Philadelphia: National Museum of American Jewish History, 1993).

43 E-mail from Julie Miller to Jeffrey Shandler, 3 August 1997.

44 *New York Times*, 2 April 1871, as cited by Davis, *The Landscape of Belief*, p. 189.

45 *The Holy Land: Drawings Made on the Spot by David Roberts with Historical Descriptions by Reverend George Croly* vol. I (London: F. G. Moon, 1842), unpaginated. Text appears on page accompanying drawing of "Jerusalem, from the Mount of Olives."

46 See Onne, *Photographic Heritage of the Holy Land*, pp. 19-20 and Davis, *The Landscape of Belief*, pp. 73-97.

47 Edward Robinson, *Biblical Researches in Palestine, Mount Sinai and Arabia Petraea*, 3 vols. (Boston: Crocker and Brewster, 1841).

48 John Kitto, *Scripture Lands; Described in a Series of Historical, Geographical, and Topographical Sketches* (London: Henry G. Bohn, 1850).

49 Morris et. al., *Bible Witnesses From Bible Lands*, esp. pp. 175ff.; see also Davis, *The Landscape of Belief*, pp. 49-51.

50 Morris et. al., *Bible Witnesses From Bible Lands*, p.5.

51 Samuel Hillel Isaacs, *The True Boundaries of the Holy Land as Described in Numbers XXXIV: 1-12* (Chicago: Jeanette Isaacs Davis, 1917), p. 8b.

52 William F. Albright, *The Archaeology of Palestine and the Bible* (New York: Revell, 1932), p. 17.

53 See Bruce Kuklick, *Puritans in Babylon: The Ancient Near East and American Intellectual Life, 1880-1930* (Princeton: Princeton University Press, 1996), pp. 5-9, 99-122.

54 Kuklick, *Puritans in Babylon*, pp. 6, 21, 122-25; Vogel, *To See a Promised Land*, pp. 185-211.

55 James Baikie, *The Glamour of Near East Excavation* (Philadelphia: J.B. Lippincott, 1923).

56 James Baikie, *The Life of The Ancient East* (New York: Macmillan, 1923), p. vii.

57 Marion Harland, *Under the Flag Of The Orient: A Woman's Vision of the Master's Land* (Philadelphia: Historical Publishing, 1897), p. 25.

58 Edward W. Said, *Orientalism* (New York: Pantheon, 1978); see also Kuklick, *Puritans in Babylon*, pp. 199-202.

59 Edwin Wilbur Rice, *Orientalisms in Bible Lands* (Philadelphia: American Sunday-School Union, 1910), p. 12.

60 See, e.g., Morris et. al., *Bible Witnesses From Bible Lands*, pp. 162-63.

61 Elkan Nathan Adler, *Jews in Many Lands* (Philadelphia: Jewish Publication Society of America, 1905), p. 45.

62 Pamphlet, "The Palestine Hebrew Culture Fund," ca. 1930, Stephen Wise Collection, Box 129, American Jewish Historical Society; Pamphlet, "Society of Friends of the 'Ohel,'" "Ohel" Hebrew Dramatic Theatre of the Jewish Workmen's Organisation in Palestine, unpaginated, American Jewish Historical Society.

63 Brochure, "Dear American Children," Series RG 17, Box 1, Folder "Child Welfare Fund," New York, Hadassah, [1937], Hadassah Archives.

64 Letter to Michael Gratz, 1763, Gratz Family Papers, Correspondence of Michael Gratz, Box 1, American Jewish Historical Society. Translated from the Hebrew by Rebecca Kobrin.

65 The most vocal advocate of the compatibility of Zionist and American ideals was Louis Brandeis. See his pamphlet, "Zionism and Patriotism," (New York: Federation of American Zionists, 1915); see also Melvin I. Urofsky, *American Zionism from Herzl to the Holocaust* (Garden City, N.Y.: Anchor Press/ Doubleday, 1975; reprint ed., Lincoln, Nebraska and London: Bison Books and University of Nebraska Press, 1995).

66 Brochure, "A Message to American Jewry," The American-Palestine Bank, Ltd., Tel Aviv, 1925, Cyrus Adler Papers, Box 18, Folder 4, Center for Judaic Studies, University of Pennsylvania Library.

67 *Rebuilding the Land of Israel* (New York: United Palestine Appeal, 1926-27), p. 31.

68 Advertisement for American Fruit Growers of Palestine, *Jewish Daily Forward*, 12 October 1920, p. 2. See also "Settle in Balfouria," *The New Palestine*, 2 March 1923, p. 156.

69 Pamphlet, "A Stitch in Time," 1934, Palestine Supplies Bureau, RG 17, Box 3, Hadassah Archives.

70 Pamphlet, "We planted, and you are invited to Reap the Benefits," Bnai Zion, ca. 1948, RG 1065, Box 2, File 11, YIVO Archives.

71 Pamphlet, "We Ring Your Bell Again," Jewish National Fund, ca. 1946, Palestine Supplies Bureau, RG 17, Box 3, Hadassah Archives.

72 Michael Berkowitz, *Zionist Culture and West European Jewry before the First World War* (Cambridge: Cambridge University Press, 1993) p. 119.

73 Simon Schama, *Landscape and Memory* (New York: Knopf, 1995), pp. 5-6.

74 Birthday card, L'Chayim To Life! series, American Greetings, Cleveland Ohio, purchased 1997.

Celebrating Zion in America
by Arthur A. Goren

Most historians have judged the success of American Zionism by two criteria: the political influence it exerted and the funds it raised. Membership numbers and the income from national campaigns have been used to measure the movement's strength and its effectiveness in the political sphere. According to these criteria, a high point was registered between 1915 and 1920, known as the "Brandeis Era." During this period, the Federation of American Zionists (which changed its name to the Zionist Organization of America [ZOA] in 1918) grew fifteen-fold, and it played a decisive role in saving the tiny Zionist settlement in Palestine during the war years. The organization's leaders, especially Louis Brandeis, were credited with President Woodrow Wilson's pro-Zionist position. A depressing low followed during the 1920s and early '30s. Membership plummeted and the income from Zionist funds fell far below expectations. Politically, the movement carried little weight in American and world Jewish affairs or in combating Britain's hostile policy toward Zionist work in Palestine. Nevertheless, in the midst of its worst slump the movement was able to tap the great reservoir of sentiment for the *yishuv*—the Jewish settlement in Palestine—when it organized protest rallies, memorial meetings and a special emergency fund following the Arab riots of 1929. With the rise of Hitler, American Zionism entered a period of growth and reached its zenith during the climactic years from 1945 to the establishment of the State of Israel in 1948. Fundraising and membership soared as most Jews accepted the Zionist position that linked the resettlement and rehabilitation of Holocaust survivors with the creation of a sovereign state in Palestine.[1]

This growing consensus went hand-in-hand with proficient organization to win over not only the great majority of American Jews but also American public opinion and a reluctant U.S. government to the cause of a Jewish state. Since the establishment of the state, assuring Israel's security has been an article of faith for American Jewry and a cornerstone of Jewish unity. At moments of great crisis, such as the 1967 Six Day War and the 1973 Yom Kippur War, the community has rallied to Israel's support in extraordinary displays of empathy and financial aid.

But Zionism's place in American Jewish life during the pre-state era should not be gauged merely by membership numbers, fundraising income, and favorable presidential pronouncements, as important as these may be. From its beginnings, American Zionism promoted a many-sided program of popular education. An ideological movement, it defined itself as the authentic expression of the collective will of the Jewish people to survive. The national home in Palestine, American Zionists declared, would not only provide a haven for the Jewish homeless; the concentration of a part of the Jewish people on its ancestral soil would also produce a cultural and spiritual renaissance that would nurture creative Jewish life everywhere.

Zionism was exceptional among American Jewish organizations in its aspiration for inclusiveness and its desire to be a mass movement. In one form or another, it endeavored to embrace Jews regardless

Arthur A. Goren is the Russell and Bettina Knapp Professor of American Jewish History at Columbia University. He is the author of *New York Jews and the Quest for Community, The American Jews,* and is presently completing a book entitled, *The Politics and Public Culture of American Jews.*

of class, belief, or gender—American-born as well as immigrants, workers as well as the middle class, secular Jews as well as members of all religious denominations. The ZOA was the most American and influential of the Zionist parties and the one that most diligently pursued the mass-movement model. The organization required minimal membership dues and published a Yiddish-language journal for many years in addition to its main periodical in English. Among the ZOA's elected presidents were Conservative rabbis Solomon Goldman and Israel Goldstein, Reform rabbis Stephen S. Wise and Abba Hillel Silver, as well as such stalwart secularists as Louis Brandeis and Louis Lipsky. In 1904, Richard Gottheil, the first president of the Federation of American Zionists, introduced the English Zionist leader Joseph Cowen at a Zionist banquet by welcoming him "on behalf of the sisters, too, for Zionism was the first movement in Judaism that freely admitted women to its deliberations."[2] Within a decade, the "sisters" had established Hadassah, the Women's Zionist Organization, which over the years became the largest of the Zionist organizations.

The smaller Zionist parties also aspired to es-

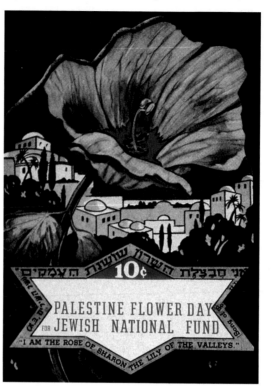

Palestine Flower Day
Jewish National Fund, ca. 1939
On flower day, which was held in the spring, donors were given a small artificial flower to wear; a miniature flag was given for a small contribution on flag day in the fall. These "tag days" brought out hundreds of active Zionists, who canvassed Jewish homes and "tagged" people on the street. The verse from the Song of Songs on this fundraising token links Zionist support with Biblical tradition.

National Museum of American Jewish History

tablish a broad base of support. The Labor Zionists whose core group, the Poale Zion Party, never numbered more than several thousand, created satellite organizations—the Jewish National Workers Alliance (a fraternal order), and the Pioneer Women. In the 1920s, Poale Zion established a Jewish trade union council and later designated the National Labor Committee for Palestine to win financial support for the Histadrut, the federation of Jewish workers in Palestine. Annual conventions launched the campaigns. In 1926, 360 delegates representing 158 organizations attended; by 1944, the yearly convention had grown to 3,000 delegates representing 1,000 organizations. The Labor Zionist organization also formed the League for Labor Palestine to attract Americanized professionals and communal leaders, and it founded the influential journal, *The Jewish Frontier*. Mizrachi, operating in the more restricted world of Orthodox Jewry, endeavored to expand its original, immigrant constituency through Jewish educational institutions, second-generation organizations like Young Israel, and an English-language periodical, *The Jewish Outlook*. It, too, had its own women's organization.

Aspiring to be a grass-roots movement, each

Zionist party created its network of neighborhood branches, chapters or local districts with a myriad of committees, city and regional councils, and a national office directed by elected officers and a professional staff. Monthly chapter meetings, periodic conferences, fundraising dinners, holiday celebrations, and concerts featuring prominent speakers and artists sent by the central office were the bread-and-butter of movement life. A house organ provided the membership with a schedule of events, directives, local reports, information on Palestine and world Jewish affairs, creating a sense of community and a political identity.

Typical of the American Zionist movement's earlier years was an "Itinerary of Speakers" notice in the January 1917 issue of *The Maccabaean*, the Federation of American Zionists monthly. Readers were informed that Shmaryahu Levin, the renowned European Zionist leader, was available for speaking engagements on behalf of the "Zionist Emergency Fund" during all of January "except for Sundays" (apparently all booked); Ben Zion Mossinsohn, the principal of the first Hebrew-speaking high school in Palestine, was concluding his Pacific tour on January 15; Menaham Sheinkin, one of the founders of Tel Aviv and active in land acquisition in Palestine, was lecturing in the greater New York area; Philip M. Raskin, a Yiddish poet and publicist recently arrived from England, was covering Alabama, Texas, Oklahoma, Kansas, Missouri and Kentucky; and the tour of Leo Motzkin, a leading European Zionist, was in the planning stage. All those mentioned in the account had arrived in the United States in the first year of the war. They were either expelled by the Turkish authorities from Palestine or refugees from the European conflict, and nearly all addressed their audiences in Yiddish. David Ben-Gurion and Yitzhak Ben-Zvi, traveling the lecture circuit for the Labor Zionists, were two other prominent Palestinian exiles. During December, *The Maccabaean* reported, 109 meetings were held "in about as many cities"; most

of the speakers were sent by Federation headquarters.[3]

The growth of the *yishuv* beginning in the 1920s, the pressing need to establish a major Zionist fundraising apparatus, and the increasing importance of American Jewry as the main source of financial aid led to frequent visits by world Zionist leaders. From London came the most eminent of them all, Chaim Weizmann, the president of the World Zionist Organization. He arrived on his first trip to the United States in April 1921, at the head of a delegation that included Albert Einstein, to launch the Keren Hayesod (the Palestine Foundation Fund). Weizmann received a welcome worthy of a chief-of-state. A launch carrying city and state officials met his ship as it entered New York harbor, a large crowd waited at the pier to accompany him to his hotel, and several days later he received the keys to the city from the mayor of New York at a ceremony at City Hall.[4] From Palestine came such labor leaders as Berl Katznelson, Golda Meyerson (Meir), David Ben-Gurion, Zalman Rubashov (Shazar), and Yosef Shprinzak to inaugurate the annual Histadrut campaign. Following a tour of thirty-four cities on behalf of the 1934 campaign, Shprinzak compared himself to a worker on a Ford assembly line, turning out the same speech in the same way that the Ford worker repeated his single task.

Understandably, the American leadership provided the lion's share of speakers, among whom rabbis were especially prominent. Several factors contributed to the strong presence of rabbis in the movement: the honored status of the minister-scholar-preacher in American life; the fact that addressing civic and philanthropic associations was part of the rabbi's communal duties; his command of English (nearly all were trained in American seminaries); and the rabbi's role as the respected spokesperson for the Jewish community in public life. Wise and Silver were the most famous of scores of rabbis who traveled the speakers' circuit. They

Zionist March
Pittsburgh, 1919

Hadassah, The Women's Zionist Organization of America

addressed conventions, mass meetings, fundraising dinners, and also held the highest offices in the Zionist movement.[5]

The capstone of the movement's organizational life was the annual convention, which brought together delegates from the entire country. Lasting two or three days, the gatherings combined inspirational oratory, policy debates, electioneering and public spectacles. Sounding the themes of Jewish solidarity, national redemption, and American patriotism, these events were directed not only at the Jewish community but at the American public as well. Two examples of such convention spectacles bear description.

The June 1918 convention of the Federation of American Zionists, held in Pittsburgh, took place at a particularly stirring time. American soldiers were joined in battle on the Western Front, British forces were advancing in Palestine after liberating Jerusalem and Judea, and only eight months earlier the British government had issued the Balfour Declaration favoring a homeland in Palestine for the Jews. The Sunday morning parade that preceded the convention's official opening originated at Zionist headquarters and ended at the Soldiers Memorial Hall, where the convention took place. Fifteen thousand people, one-fourth of the Jewish population of Pittsburgh, were in the marching line. The parade included fifteen bands and contingents representing all the Zionist parties, fraternal orders and youth groups. The newspaper accounts took special note of the women's organizations that participated. The women wore sashes decorated with the flags of the allies and marched under the banner, "Mothers of Democracy." One group of "Jewish war mothers" wore service flags on their dress. Leading the parade, *The Maccabaean* reported, was a "squad of Jewish *shomerim*," the famed watchmen who guarded the Zionist settlement. The author of the report, himself a Palestinian Jew, wrote that the *shomerim* lent to "the imposing demonstration a Palestinian color. The white head-dress and costume, the manner of riding, the weapons, stirred the fancy and brought living greetings from the hills of Judaea, from Carmel and Tabor, from Shefelah and Sharon, where the fallen are reposing and the living are struggling." Two hundred thousand people, most of them non-Jews, watched the three-hour-long march. The blue and white Zionist flag flew on top of city hall.[6]

In May 1920, a crowd estimated between 50,000 and 100,000 people marched along a five-mile route from lower Manhattan to Central Park in conjunction with an "extraordinary Zionist convention" convened in New York to mark the award of the Palestine mandate to Great Britain (the San Remo Declaration of April 24, 1920). Behind the banner, "*Geulah*—Redemption," flag-bearers carried the American, Zionist and British flags. Two buses of wounded Jewish veterans followed, and behind them were Jewish survivors of the legendary "Lost Battalion" of New York's 77th ("Metropolitan") Division. Next in order came veterans of the Jewish Legion who fought in Palestine, American Legionnaires, and Hadassah women dressed in blue and white. Twenty-seven sections "representing all Jewish organizations" filled out the line of march. Such festive occasions—uniformed and costumed formations, identifiable by their organizational banners and parading in unison to the sound of the bands and the cheers of thousands of bystanders— reflected the popular American practice of civic celebration. However, the parade as pageant rather than as protest became a regular feature of American

Jewish public life only after 1965, when the first Israel Independence Day parade sponsored by the American Zionist Youth Foundation was held along New York's Fifth Avenue.[7]

Instead, the "mass meeting" was the prevailing mode of rallying public support. Held in the heart of the city—in the public square, concert hall or sports arena—the mass meeting was attended by thousands and reported to hundreds of thousands more through the press and later by radio and television. Invariably, a battery of speakers that included representatives of the sponsoring organizations, key political figures, and non-Jewish Zionist supporters, delivered messages of approval or protest depending on the circumstances. Often the meeting concluded with a set of resolutions adopted by acclamation.[8]

This was the case with the enormous rally held on November 2, 1930, in New York's Madison Square Garden. Called to mark the thirteenth anniversary of the Balfour Declaration, to protest Britain's White Paper restricting Jewish immigration and land acquisition in Palestine, and to affirm a united Jewry's determination to support the *yishuv*, the rally attracted a crowd of 50,000. Twenty-five thousand people packed into the Garden and an equal number gathered in the neighboring streets. Among the speakers were Lieutenant Governor Herbert H. Lehman; Felix Frankfurter, the Harvard Law School professor who had served as legal adviser to the Zionist delegation to the Paris Peace Conference; Representative Hamilton Fish, Jr., who had sponsored the Congressional resolution in 1922 endorsing the Jewish national home; and Felix M. Warburg, the banker-philanthropist and key non-Zionist figure in the recently established Jewish Agency for Palestine. Robert Szold, representing the ZOA, chaired the meeting, and speakers for the Labor Zionists, Mizrachi, and the American Jewish Congress greeted the assembly. Simultaneously, in twenty other cities, 700,000 people attended mass meetings in what *The New Palestine* described as "the greatest nation-wide series of meetings that has ever been sponsored by American Jewry. . . . Practically every city in the land provided a replica of what took place at Madison Square Garden."

The 1930 Balfour Day protest meetings were matched and possibly surpassed at other critical junctures. One such instance was the wave of protests during September and October 1945, following Britain's rejection of President Harry Truman's request that 100,000 displaced persons (DPs) be allowed to emigrate to Palestine; another was the reaction to the British Army's arrest of the *yishuv's* leadership in July 1946.[9]

In addition to the pageant-parade and the protest meeting, the Zionists elaborated a range of other forms of public celebrations. The Jewish holiday calendar was an obvious source of inspiration. The Labor Zionists invented the "third seder," later borrowed by other organizations, which took place some time during the Passover week. The content of the "third seder" changed from place to place, but the format remained similar: a festive meal, speeches, an artistic program, and in some cases a secularized, abbreviated *haggadah* inspired by the new Passover *haggadot* of the kibbutzim. In some of the larger cities, the "third seder" was appropriated by the annual Histadrut

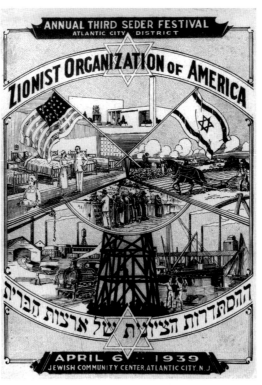

Annual Third Seder Festival
Zionist Organization of America
Atlantic City, New Jersey, 1939

YIVO Institute for Jewish Research Library

campaign. Held at a major hotel or resort, the festive Passover meal was interspersed with Palestinian pioneer and Yiddish folk songs. Next came speakers who "greeted" the assembled in the name of the host organizations and "prepared" the audience for the "honored guest." The seder at the Hotel Astor in New York, held on April 17, 1938, was attended by 2,500 guests who paid $15 each. Advertised as the "sixth annual third seder," the highlight of the evening was the appearance of two distinguished speakers: Albert Einstein, who spoke briefly in German, and Herbert Morrison, the British Labor Party leader. They were preceded by, among others, Golda Meyerson, representing the Histadrut; David Pinski, the Yiddish playwright and President of the Jewish National Workers Alliance; Abraham Cahan, editor of the *Jewish Daily Forward*; and Hayim Greenberg, editor of the Labor Zionist *Jewish Frontier*. Among the artists who took part were the tenor Jan Peerce, the choreographer and dancer Benjamin Zemach, the cellist Milah Wolerson, and the Jewish folk singer, Isa Kremer. Moshe Natanson, cantor of the Reconstructionist Society for the Advancement of Judaism and one of the popularizers of the Palestinian folk song in America, led the gathering in communal singing. New York's 1940 "third seder" attracted twice as many participants and took place simultaneously at the Astor and Commodore hotels. Senator William King of Utah was the featured speaker at both affairs. (The Yiddish newspaper *The Day* reported the event in dramatic terms, declaring: "Senator King, Accomplishments of the Jewish Workers of Eretz Israel are a greater miracle than the Exodus from Egypt.") The centerpiece of the artistic program was a "living *haggadah*"—"From Slavery to Freedom"—directed by Zvee Scooler of the Yiddish stage, with music by Herz Ruben and lyrics by the Hebrew poet, essayist and translator Abraham Regelson.

Purim, traditionally the occasion for revelry and charity balls, was a Hadassah favorite. The organization was founded on Purim, and the founders named it Hadassah, the Hebrew name of Esther, the heroine of the Purim story.[10] However, the transformation of Hanukkah from a minor home ritual into a public festival in the service of Zionism is especially noteworthy. For the Zionists, the Maccabaean uprising—the victory of a band of zealous Jewish fighters over the superior Syrian host—provided the sublime symbol of heroism. In the name of the pure faith and the nation's honor, Judah Maccabee led the struggle for the restoration of Jewish independence. Hanukkah, the celebration of the rededication of the Temple, became the occasion for linking the Maccabees of old with the new Maccabees, the *halutzim* (Zionist pioneers), who were redeeming the land of Israel with their labor. By 1920, the *halutz* and the concept of *halutziut* (pioneering) came to represent the core ideal of Zionism. The image of young, courageous pioneers—who had left behind careers or university studies, placing the welfare of their people above

Ticket to the Grand Ball of the Downtown Zionist District
New York, 1927

National Museum of American Jewish History

private ambition—became the central myth of Zionism and the great hope of fulfilling its goals.

Celebrating Hanukkah in America was also popular for pragmatic reasons. It coincided with the Christmas-New Year holiday season and its round of festivities. Zionists were not averse to running New Year's Eve dances. Holding an annual Hanukkah "concert and ball" was especially popular. One such affair, sponsored by the Labor Zionists in New York on December 24, 1916, included a performance by the Poale Zion Chorus and a set of *tableaux vivants* representing "Jewish reality and ideals." Beginning with a scene entitled, "By the Rivers of Babylon," the series concluded with "Herzl's Dream," an image inspired by E.M. Lilien's famous photograph of Theodor Herzl at Basel. The highlight of the evening was the screening of *Life in the Holy Land*, a documentary film about Palestine. Produced by the Misrach Company in time to be premiered at the 1913 World Zionist Congress in Vienna, the film included "160 pictures from Palestine" and featured the 30th anniversary celebration of the village of Gedera.[11]

By the 1930s, the local "concert and ball" format was transformed into a city-wide extravaganza that required a central public location. In New York, the preferred site was Madison Square Garden. The program of the third New York Hanukkah festival, held on December 24, 1932, offers some notion of the mix of sacred history, Zionism, popular entertainment, and the inevitable keynote speaker that had become fairly standard. A choir of 120 voices offered excerpts from Handel's *Judas Maccabaeus* and a medley of Palestinian "choral chants"; a soloist presented "songs appropriate to the splendor of the Maccabean tradition" as well as "new melodies of the Palestinian *halutzim*"; Harry Hershfield, the well-known comic-strip artist and popular master of ceremonies, introduced a galaxy of stars that included Eddie Cantor, Ethel Merman, and Jack Pearl. Lieutenant Governor Lehman delivered the "Hanukkah address." (The year before, Albert Einstein had been the main speaker.) In 1933, two performances of the "Gala Maccabaean Festival" were needed to meet the demand for tickets. In addition to "the usual program of Broadway stars and radio and screen celebrities," a cast of 500 actors and dancers and a symphony orchestra presented a "depiction of modern Jewish life in Palestine." The performance included a "*halutz* ballet" expressing "the ideals and aspirations of the Jewish pioneer."[12]

The extraordinary success of Chicago's 1932 Hanukkah Festival is notable for the role played by an imaginative Zionist functionary turned producer, who used the occasion to unite the entire Jewish community "under one banner." Meyer Weisgal, invited to serve as executive director for the moribund Midwest Zionist region, wrote:

> The Zionist field in Chicago was strewn with dry bones and a thousand speeches were not going to revive them. . . . I realized at once that in these circumstances pedestrian Zionist propaganda and routine education, however well intentioned, would produce no effect. There had to be, first, a reawakening, and I turned to the performing arts—music, drama, spectacle. . . . The holiday of the Maccabees was not far off, and I decided to arrange a great spectacle telling the story of the ancient struggle. The highlight of the evening was to be: *no speeches!*[13]

The banner line announcing the Hanukkah Festival, scheduled for the second day of Hanukkah, December 25, 1932, read: "A Colossal Program which Combines a Tremendous Pageant, A Concert, a Dance, and a Gala Performance—Cast of 1,000." Weisgal succeeded in winning the cooperation of scores of Jewish organizations whom he listed as co-sponsors with the Zionist Organization; he also activated several thousand Hebrew school children and members of youth organizations, who served as dancers and singers in the mass scenes. Weeks of rehearsals were required to prepare the novices. Weisgal quipped that, for every youngster who participated in the pageant, he could count on selling a dozen tickets to family, cousins and friends. 27,000 people filled Chicago Stadium and watched the story of the Maccabean victory unfold. In the climactic scene, the rededication of the Temple, "temple dancers and daughters of Zion appeared from six different entrances, moving toward stage center. A great candelabra [sic] cast bright light over the scene." (The pre-festival advertisement announced that Maurie Sherman's Dance Orchestra would provide three hours of dancing—one may assume, in the light of the candelabrum.)[14]

Another Weisgal triumph was the most grandiose spectacle of all. It took place on July 3, 1933, at Soldier Field, Chicago, marking "Jewish Day" at the Chicago World's Fair. Both the Zionist Organization of America and B'nai B'rith scheduled their annual conventions in Chicago to coincide with "Jewish Day," and Weisgal brought Chaim Weizmann from London to address the grand affair. 130,000 spectators filled the stadium to watch *Romance of a People*, with its cast of 6,200, depict the 4,000-year saga of the Jews. The final episode, "The New Liberation," consisted of two sequences: America—the mass unfurling of the Stars and Stripes; and Palestine—throngs of young people dressed as Zionist pioneers running on stage singing the *halutz* folk song, *"Anu banu artza liv'not u'lihibanot ba"* (We have come to the land to build it and be rebuilt)." The *halutzim* then broke into a *hora,* the fiery circle dance they made famous. Two days later a repeat performance played to an audience of 75,000, this time cosponsored by the *Chicago Daily Tribune* and an interfaith committee. Indeed, the ecumenical interest that the pageant elicited was remarkable.

Romance of a People moved to New York City in September. Rained out at the Polo Grounds, the pageant was relocated to the Kingsbridge Armory in the Bronx for a run of twenty-one performances before going on tour to Philadelphia, Detroit, and Cleveland. Everywhere the press gave the pageant massive coverage, depicting it as the magnificent response of a proud and ancient people— the people of the book—to Nazi barbarities.[15]

"Rebuilding the Land of Israel,"
New York: United Palestine Appeal, 1926-27

National Museum of American Jewish History

United Jewish Appeal (combining the United Palestine Appeal and the Joint Distribution Committee) presented the Jewish homeland in Palestine as the best hope for Germany's Jews. In September, 1934, the combined appeals—undoubtedly impressed by the success of the Hanukkah celebrations and the *Romance of a People*— produced the first "Night of Stars." The ticket sales were earmarked "for refugees and Palestine." An "Amusement Division," part of the fundraising strategy of organizing by business sectors, recruited Broadway, Hollywood, and radio artists to donate their time. Among the stars who appeared were Irving Berlin, Eddie Cantor, Al Jolson, George Jessel, Jack Pearl, and Sigmund Romberg, and the heavyweight boxing champion of the world, Primo Canera. Colonel Jacob Ruppert gave the use of Yankee Stadium gratis.[16]

The rise of Hitler and the tide of mass protest meetings across the nation stimulated fundraising activity as well. When they managed to collaborate, the United Palestine Appeal (combining the Keren Hayesod and the Jewish National Fund) and the

In succeeding years the United Palestine Appeal became the sole sponsor of the "Night of Stars," the date was fixed for sometime in November, and the venue moved to Madison Square Garden. The roll of artists who contributed their services grew, the staging became more elaborate, and the voluntary support structure expanded. A general committee and an executive committee coordinated the work of the women's division, trades council, and program, production, public relations, ticket distribution, and yearbook committees. The 1937 affair featured Paul Muni re-enacting the courtroom scene from the recent film *The Life of Emile Zola*, in which he played the title role. George M. Cohan brought together a group of older composers and performers in a segment entitled, "Tin Pan Alley on Parade." Arthur Murray, the "noted dance authority," staged "his conception of the Big Apple." However, the evening opened on a highbrow note: Alexander Smallens conducted a full-sized symphony orchestra and a choir of 250 voices. The speakers made their appeals for funds in a "pre-program" time slot, evidently so as not to disturb the flow of the entertainment portion of the program.[17]

The featured artist of the 1939 "Night of Stars" was violinist Jascha Heifetz. (An advance story noted that Heifetz had postponed a Carnegie Hall recital in order to take part in the program.) Also participating were the bandleaders Benny Goodman, Louis Armstrong and Eddie Duchin, and from Hollywood, Louise Rainer (who recreated a scene from the film *The Good Earth*), Jimmy Durante, Dick Powell and Joan Blondell. Through its broad list of invited performers, the producers emphasized the "non-sectarian" dimension of the affair. Cognizant of the public's wartime anxieties, the arrangement committee announced that the well-known news broadcasters Raymond Gram Swing, Gabriel Heatter, and Johannes Steele, would provide the audience with a summary of their evening newscasts. At the close of the five-hour calvacade of entertainment, the audience received pledge cards in the name of the "greatest artists of stage, screen, radio and opera to contribute to the United Palestine Appeal" and help

bring "the thousands of homeless and oppressed men and women" to Palestine. Distinguished public figures who filled the box seats—their names were announced in the press—added a prestigious note to the festivities. The annual "Night of Stars" was also broadcast on radio.[18]

During the 1920s, films, most of which were commissioned by the Jewish National Fund and the Keren Hayesod, became an important vehicle for presenting Zionist accomplishments in Palestine to the public. Usually, they were used to supplement a speaker or round out a cultural program. Only with the feature-length sound documentary *Land of Promise*, which opened at New York's Astor Theater in November 1935 and was distributed nationally, was the full potential of the medium realized. The *New York Times* film critic praised the "noble, excellently photographed and skillfully edited film record of the rebuilding of the Jewish homeland in Palestine." He was especially moved by the contrast between the Palestine before and after the "Jews flocked back to the homeland." On the one hand, there were the scenes of Arabs in their "medieval marketplaces" and "sad-faced" *fellahin* in the fields flailing wheat; on the other hand, the camera captured the bustling life in Tel Aviv, Jerusalem, and Haifa—scenes of construction work, industry, relaxing on the beach, and a concert in the Hebrew University's amphitheater on Mt. Scopus. The *yishuv* was presented as a thriving, modern society both culturally and economically.[19]

But the true heroes of the film were the *halutzim*. The *Times* critic described their initial appearance in the film: "Suddenly, the lens is opened wide upon a dancing, singing group of young men and women on the foredeck of a liner, coming to give new life to the century old city [sic], coming to water its fields, run its factories, build its homes. The effect upon the audience is electric."[20] *Land of Promise* presented the *halutzim* hard at work—drilling for water and directing its flow to arid fields made fertile, spraying the groves, and plowing and then harvesting with modern farm machinery. Women worked alongside men in construction, field work, and milking cows.

Halutzim also celebrated the fruits of their labor. The camera caught the annual harvest festival in Haifa—a grand parade of wagons of produce, floats and folk dancers—and a scene of communal singing in the dining hall of the kibbutz, in which the composer Daniel Sambursky teaches his "Emek Song," the theme song of the film.[21]

The Zionists took full advantage of the opportunity for publicity at the film's premiere. None other than Albert Einstein headed the distinguished list of guests who attended the opening ceremonies, which were broadcast on the radio. The *New Palestine* described the "thrilling scene" when a group of "American halutzim" arrived from their training farm in New Jersey for the event. Dressed in white shirts with pitchforks and rakes on their shoulders, they entered the lobby as "hundreds of people cheered and cam-

eramen eagerly sought to photograph them." The blue and white banner across Broadway advertising the film gave "poignant evidence to all who pass that Palestine has become a vital reality in Jewish life."[22]

The official opening of the Jewish Palestine Pavilion at the New York World's Fair on May 28, 1939, was another landmark mass event. The ceremonies were held in the Court of Peace, as the Pavilion's premises were too small to contain the opening-day crowd. The event turned into a demonstration against the British White Paper, which declared an end to Jewish immigration to Palestine in five years time. One-hundred thousand people attended the opening, and an array of Zionist leaders and public figures spoke. Einstein—Zionism's icon of Jewish genius, virtue, and love of Zion, and the most famous of all German refugees—was given the honor of dedicating the Pavilion. And, after much wrangling, the Jewish flag was permitted to fly from the "bridge of flags," despite the opposition of the

Palestine Maccabees vs. Pennsylvania All Stars
Philadelphia, 1936
This sporting event promoted Zionism in the popular context of American athletics.

Collection of Peter H. Schweitzer

British embassy and the U.S. State Department.[23]

The Jewish Palestine exhibition ran for nearly two years, and over 2,000,000 people visited the Pavilion. It became a site for pilgrimages from cities outside of New York. Organizations sponsored special days for ceremonial gatherings. "Hadassah Day," for example, took place several weeks after the opening. Eddie Cantor was honored for his service to Youth Aliyah, the Yemenite dancer Naomi Aleh-Leaf performed the traditional dances of her community, the Hadassah National Board met in the courtyard, and a luncheon followed at Cafe Tel Aviv.[24]

Those who visited the Pavilion entered the Hall of Transformation and ascended a broad staircase that symbolized Jewish immigration to Palestine. Dominating the staircase was "a heroic statue of a *halutz*," and behind the statue a sweeping photomural depicted "the march of the *halutzim*." On the right was a mural showing a huge map of Palestine; opposite were enlarged photographs that "depicted the transformation of swamps into healthful settlements, of rocky hills into a thriving colony, and sand dunes into the modern metropolis of Tel Aviv."[25]

The parades, films, pageants and exhibitions generally projected the image of an American Jewry united in its support of the Zionist enterprise. However, in two instances, maverick Zionists denounced the Jewish and Zionist establishments and called on the rank-and-file of American Jews to reject their leadership. In March 1943 and again in September 1946, Hollywood sceenwriter Ben Hecht joined forces with the Peter Bergson group—militant young Palestinian Zionists who arrived in the United States at the outbreak of the war—to produce the pageants *We Will Never Die* and *A Flag is Born*.

The "Bergson Boys" had been educated in Revisionist Zionism and were members of its underground affiliate, the Irgun or Etzel (the Hebrew acronym for National Military Organization). They had come to the United States to raise funds for arms for the Irgun and to finance the "illegal" immigration of Jews from Europe. Revisionism, which championed a Jewish state on "both sides of the Jordan," advocated an aggressive policy in dealing with the British and Arabs. The movement seceded from the World Zionist Organization to pursue its own political strategy, unencumbered by democratic process. In 1944, Britain's strict enforcement of immigration policy in the face of Germany's extermination program led Menahem Begin, the commander of the Irgun, to declare a "revolt" against the British. In the *yishuv*, a legacy of hostility that sometimes included physical violence divided the Revisionist-Irgun camp and the Labor-Haganah majority. Financed and covertly controlled by the Jewish Agency/Zionist Organization, the Haganah was recognized by most Jews as the "official" defense force of the *yishuv*. Labor Zionists stigmatized the Revisionist as schismatics and extremists; the Revisionists labeled the Zionist leadership "appeasers."[26]

In America, the Bergsonites established front organizations for political lobbying, propaganda and fundraising, creating new ones as circumstances warranted: American Friends of a Jewish Palestine (1939-1941); Committee for a Jewish Army (1941-1943); Emergency Committee to Rescue the Jewish People in Europe (1943-1945); Hebrew Committee of National Liberation; the American League for a Free Palestine; the Repatriation Fund (1946); and the Palestine Resistance Fund (1944-1947). The Zionist establishment viewed the Bergson Group's independent political activity, the effectiveness of its publicity, its anti-British militancy, and its growing number of sympathizers as a menace.[27]

In the first of his pageants, *We Will Never Die*, billed as "A Memorial to the Two Million Jewish Dead of Europe," Hecht mounted a three-fold assault on the indifference of the free world to the mass murder of European Jewry and the collusion through inaction of the American government and the Jewish establishment. Sponsored by the Committee for a

Jewish Army, the pageant opened on March 9, 1943, in Madison Square Garden, and it was repeated in Washington, Philadelphia, Chicago, Boston and Los Angeles. Eleanor Roosevelt, who attended the Washington performance, reviewed the pageant favorably in her newspaper column—a major public relations coup for the pageant's sponsors.[28]

When *A Flag is Born* opened in September, 1946, the first stage of the battle for Palestine was at its height. The clandestine movement of refugees from the DP camps to Palestine was well underway, and the deportation of "illegal" immigrants to Cyprus had begun. The Haganah and the Irgun, in a rare moment of collaboration, responded by attacking British police stations, bridges, radar stations, and railroads. The British countered with arms searches, mass arrests, and deportations to detention camps in Africa. The Irgun returned to its tactics of reprisal. On July 22, it blew up a wing of the King David Hotel, which housed British government offices. The resulting heavy loss of life exacerbated the complex, vexatious negotiations that the Zionist leadership was conducting.

Hecht's play, a melodrama of the first order, plied a number of painful questions that he used to justify the hardline political stand of the Irgun: the only solution to the Jewish problem was a "Free Palestine," attainable only by fighting the British. But first, Hecht felt compelled to make his accounting with America's Jews, to turn the screw of guilt: "Where were you—Jews? Where were you when the killing was going on? When the six million were burned and buried alive . . . We didn't hear any voice. There was no voice. You Jews of America! . . . Strong Jews, rich Jews . . . . Where was your cry of rage that would have filled the world and stopped the fires? Nowhere!" The accusing voice was that of the despairing David, a young survivor of the death camps, played by Marlon Brando.[29]

The dénouement of *A Flag Is Born* comes in a vision. David is beckoned by three soldiers of the Jewish underground, carrying submachine guns, urging him to "cross the bridge" and join them in the fight. "We fling no more prayers or tears at the world. We fling bullets. The new Jewish voice speaks from out of these guns." The play ends with the line, "Come David, help us give birth to a flag." David improvises a Zionist flag from a *tallis* (prayer shawl) and a Star of David, and, to the sound of "Hatikvah" and the rattle of guns, approaches the bridge. The curtain falls.[30]

After playing for fifteen weeks on Broadway, *A Flag Is Born* went on the road to Chicago, Detroit, Philadelphia, Baltimore and Boston. Bergson's American League for a Free Palestine was the official producer and benefited from its financial success, not to mention its political impact. A sponsoring committee that included Marc Blitzstein, Lion Feuchtwanger, Leonard Bernstein, Mayor William O'Dwyer, and Eleanor Roosevelt, among many others, endowed the play with credibility, as did a cast that included Paul Muni and Celia Adler in the lead roles. Above all, *A Flag Is Born* was a political manifesto. The League's motto, "It is 1776 in Palestine," was especially effective. Used frequently by League speakers, it is also alluded to in the background inset of the play's souvenir program: three Revolutionary War soldiers with fife and drum march in tandem with the three Jewish freedom fighters in the foreground.[31]

The stage bill included League leaflets asserting the movement's positions and appealing for contributions to the "Repatriation Fund." Monies would be used to "evacuate displaced persons from pogrom areas to Palestine." At the conclusion of the play, the theater manager announced to the audience that money pledged that evening would be telegraphed overseas that night in order to purchase ships to transport Jewish refugees to Palestine. (One informant estimated that the League netted a million dollars from the production.) Only much later did the League purchase, outfit, and dispatch a single ship, appropriately named the "Ben Hecht." Caught

A Flag is Born
by Ben Hecht and Kurt Weill
New York, 1946

Weill-Lenya Research Center,
Kurt Weill Foundation for Music, New York

by the British on March 7, 1947, its 600 refugee passengers were interned in Cyprus.[32]

The play ignited a storm of controversy. The bluster and bravado did strike a responsive chord among many. But the play was inseparable from its sponsors, and the League's claims often enraged those who knew the gaping distance between rhetoric and reality. Of sixty-five ships that sailed for Palestine between the end of World War II and the founding of the State of Israel, sixty-four were organized by the *Mosad le-aliyah bet*, a branch of the Haganah. However, until the spring of 1947, the Jewish Agency refused to admit its responsibility for the *aliyah bet* operations for political and security reasons.[33] From time to time, when news broke of an *aliyah bet* ship reaching Palestine in the face of the Jewish Agency's silence, the uninformed credited the League and the Irgun.

In the battle of paid advertisements, the Bergson Group led with Hecht's strong pen. Perhaps his best-known copy appeared in mid-May 1947, under the caption, "Letter to the Terrorists of Palestine." He began, "My Brave Friends," and in the most provocative paragraph wrote:

> Every time you blow up a British arsenal, or wreck a British jail, or send a British railroad sky high, or rob a British bank or let go with your guns and bombs at the British betrayers and invaders of your homeland, the Jews of America make a little holiday in their hearts."[34]

The "wall of silence" was broken in a stinging attack on Hecht, using the medium in which he so excelled. Habonim, the Labor Zionist youth movement—scores of whose members had volunteered to man the *aliyah bet* ships—broke "Zionist discipline" and acknowledged the Zionist establishment's role in *aliyah bet*. Habonim's purpose was to reverse the increasing public sympathy for the League. In February 1947, the League had demanded the dissolution of the Jewish Agency, which it accused of "appeasement and collaboration with the British oppressors." Habonim placed full-page advertisements in *PM*, the *New York Post* and *The Nation* under the banner, "Action by Haganah! This is Resistance." One column listed the names of thirty Haganah ships and the number of immigrants they had brought; ships that the British "do not know about" went unmentioned. The acrimony between the rival groups is suggested by the following excerpts from the newspaper advertisement:

There are new play-boys in America,
They play with Jewish blood.
The thrills of Hollywood are no longer sharp enough,

They need lustier excitement, bolder showmanship,
The play-boys are lucky; they have a subject
worthy of their wits—the Jewish struggle.

* * * *

The Haganah is Jewish resistance.
The battle in Palestine is not being fought by
     irresponsible bands,
Nor are the dwellers in the DP camps being led on
     the path to Palestine by publicity-hounds.
It is the workers of the Haganah who guide the
     Jewish survivors across the steep
     mountain passes to the Mediterranean.
It is the sea-men of the Haganah who steer the
     "illegal" ships.
It is the swimmers of the Haganah who bear the
     refugees ashore.
It is the soldiers of the Haganah who defend the crags
     of Galilee and the plains of the Emek.
The smart alecks do not do it; the Irgunists do not
     do it; the high-pressure hucksters, who try
     to cash in on the credit, do not do it.[35]

Copies of the advertisement were distributed to meetings of the League, to the presidents of all Hadassah chapters, and to key districts of the ZOA.

The contributions brought in by the advertisement enabled Habonim to experiment with another medium in the battle over public opinion. In the fall of 1947, the organization produced a record album of folk songs, *Haganah, Songs of the Jewish Underground*. The notes on the inside cover explained: "A great struggle will produce great folk music. In our own time we have witnessed the birth of immortal songs that have sprung from the Russian revolution, the Spanish Civil War, the concentration camps of Germany, and now from the Jewish pioneers of Palestine."

The album featured the Italian-trained soloist Dov Arres and the musicianship and technical production were of a high order. Each of the folk songs was sung in English translation followed by the Hebrew original, thus making them accessible to the American public. The order of the selections traced the saga of "the return to the land": first, "*Hora* in the Foreign Land;" second, "*Ma'apilim*," describing the *aliyah bet* ship approaching the coast of Palestine in the dark of the night; third, the "Song of Chanita," the northernmost border kibbutz; and fourth, the "Palmach" hymn of the elite unit of the Haganah. The album concluded with a reading of Nathan Alterman's poem, "To the Captain of the Hannah Szenes," which was circulated *sub rosa* in Palestine when the British censor refused to allow its publication. "To the Captain" was a tribute to the Italian sea captain who had successfully run the British blockade.[36]

The British withdrawal from Palestine, the declaration of a state on May 15, 1948, and the invasion of the Arab armies unified American Jewry as never before, although scars remained among the active Zionists of all shades. Beyond protest meetings, parades, and pageants, the everyday life of a devoted Zionist family encompassed a host of activities that tied it to Zion. For the young, there were those Hebrew schools where Jewish educators emphasized Hebrew as a living language and drew upon the cultural life of the *yishuv* to enrich the curriculum. Zionist summer camps (some run as miniature kibbutzim), youth organizations, and community centers popularized the folk songs, dances, holidays, and "lifestyle" of the Jewish homeland, and especially of the heroic *halutzim*. Young Judea, for example, the largest of the Zionist youth organizations, published an educational program that had the members simulate being a *halutz* at their club activities. The authors of the program wrote:

We say to our Young Judaean, 'This year BE CHALUTZIM! Go to Eretz Israel, found your colony.' . . . We hope that many of them will be challenged and inspired with the dynamic urge to go to Palestine

SONG AND **SOIL**
שירי המולדת

PALESTINIAN FOLK SONGS
Sung by the
UNITED SYNAGOGUE CHORUS
Directed by
MARTIN BERKOWITZ
Foreword by
LEONARD BERNSTEIN

Record album, *Song and Soil/Shirei Ha-moledet*
Sung by United Synagogue Chorus, n.d.
The foreword to this album, written by Leonard Bernstein, proclaims, "The Jews of Palestine are
producing a culture all their own, rooted in its own soil, proud of itself, strongly and unashamedly
Eastern. It is full of power, healthy naiveté, and directness. Its folk art speaks out for
all the world to perceive."

YIVO Institute for Jewish Research Archives

and to became builders. But we need Chalutzim here, too.[37]

The popularity of the folk song as a way of identifying emotionally with the *yishuv* is illuminating. Early in the movement's history, the songs of the pioneers were familiar to the Zionist membership. In 1919, the musicologist Joseph Reider described the "folksong of the New Palestine" as "firm and manly, joyous and hopeful, brimful of verve and resilience, elasticity and sinuosity and buoyancy and warmth." Abraham W. Binder, who conducted the Hadassah Choral Union in 1916, the first chorus to sing "Palestinian folks songs in America," published the initial volume of his series of *New Palestinian Folk Songs* in 1924. His song books were used extensively in religious schools. One Jewish educator recalls that "many youngsters made their first contact with Zionist ideas through the new Palestinian music." At Zionist gatherings and even at conferences of Jewish social workers, the informal session of "Palestinian" folk song and folk dance, especially the *hora* of the *halutzim*, was always uplifting.

The folk dance went hand in hand with the folk song, although it took longer for an indigenous style to develop. In 1934 when Jacob Weinberger's full-length folk opera, *The Pioneers (Hechalutz)*, had its world premiere in New York City, the *New York Times* critic praised Dvora Lapson's choreography: "[Her] ballet, based on the Palestinian Hora, spirited and well composed, was quite the brightest spot of the entire production."[38]

During the 1930s and following the war's end, a stream of performers from Palestine as well as American Jewish artists visiting Palestine enriched Jewish Palestine's influence on Jewish music, folk song and dance. Yemenite singers Bracha Zefira and Sara Osnath Ha-Levy concertized extensively in the 1930s, and after 1945 Shoshana Damari and Yaffa Yarkoni toured in the United States frequently. Bracha Zefira's recordings appeared in the mid-1930s on the Columbia label, and by the 1940s, other record albums appeared, including *New Songs of Palestine* arranged by Binder and *Favorite Songs of Israel for Home and School* produced by the Palestine Art Corporation for the Hebrew Teachers Union. The Hechalutz Organization and Massada, the Young Zionist Organization, issued *Songs the Chalutzim Sing*, with arrangements by Aaron Copland, Kurt Weill, Paul Dessau, Darius Milhaud, and Erich Walter Sternberg.[39]

Jewish art from Palestine was introduced to the public in occasional exhibitions. The most energetic of the Palestinian art entrepreneurs was Boris Schatz, the pioneering founder of the Bezalel School of Arts and Crafts in Jerusalem. The students of the school, trained in art as well as handicrafts, produced work in bronze, silver, and olivewood which Schatz brought to the United States. In 1914, an exhibition of Bezalel work in New York ran for eight days, before moving to Philadelphia, Baltimore, Chicago, Cincinnati, and St. Louis. Eliahu Lewin-Epstein, one of the founders of Rehovot and the representative of Carmel Wines in the United States, became Bezalel's distributor. In 1926, Schatz organized a second exhibition of Bezalel work, which took place at New York's Grand Central Palace before touring other cities. He returned to Jerusalem with a number of commissions from American synagogues for religious artifacts. Reuven Rubin, who had studied for a time at Bezalel and then in Paris, exhibited his paintings in New York in 1920. On his second visit in 1928, the Zionist press hailed him as the *yishuv's* outstanding painter, Palestine's Gauguin.[40]

For committed Zionists, the movement was a way of life, beginning at home where the *mezuzah* on the door and the Sabbath candlesticks and wine on the table might well have been *tozereth ha-aretz*, products of the land. Beyond the home, the committee work planning communal events, the events themselves, and the compulsion to attend the meetings, dinners, demonstrations or victory celebrations, stiffened the sense of purpose and direction of American Zionism. Zionists perceived themselves as the salt of the Jewish earth and as the only ones whose movement could once and for all "solve the Jewish problem"; they alone could rescue fellow Jews from the catastrophe that awaited them in the lands of oppression or, when that catastrophe ensued, save the survivors and prevent it from ever happening again. If the act of redemption was taking place two oceans away, American Zionists were there vicariously. They could march proudly in parades carrying the Zionist flag, sing "Hatikvah" at every meeting, dance the *hora* while singing *"Anu banu artza,"* and, of course, raise the funds to build the land in a host of imaginative and effective ways. To be a committed Zionist in America was to be linked intimately to every phase of the *yishuv's* idyllic life, where all were idealists and heroes.

Notes

[1] For an overview of American Zionism, see Naomi Cohen, *American Jews and the Zionist Idea* (New York: KTAV, 1975). Melvin I. Urofsky offers a detailed narrative account in *American Zionism from Herzl to the Holocaust* (Garden City, New York: Anchor Press, 1975), and *We Are One! American Jewry and Israel* (Garden City, New York: Anchor Press, 1978).

[2] *The Maccabaean,* 6:6 (June 1904), p. 293.

[3] *The Maccabaean,* 30:1 (January 1917), pp. 141, 142. For an announcement of a "mass meeting" to introduce Motzkin and Mossinsohn at Cooper Union in New York, see *ibid.,* 28:3 (March 1916), pp. 51, 71.

[4] *New York Times,* 2 April 1921, p. 11; 3 April 1921, p. 1; 6 April 1921, p. 1; 26 April 1924. p. 1.

[5] Samuel Halperin, *The Political World of American Zionism* (Detroit: Wayne State University Press, 1961), pp. 97-100, 103-111; Ilan Kaisar, "Labor Zionism in the U.S.A.—Poale-Zion—Zeir-Zion—1931-1947" [Hebrew], Ph.D. diss., Hebrew University, 1994, pp. 88, 210-11.

[6] *Der Tog,* 23 June 1918, p. 1; 24 June 1918, p. 1; *The Maccabaean,* 31:8 (August 1918), pp. 245, 253; *Jewish Criterion* [Pittsburgh], 28 June 1918, p. 1.

[7] *The Maccabaean,* 33:5 (June 1920), p. 193; *New York Times,* 11 May 1920, p. 25; 12 May 1920, p. 16; *Der Tog,* 12 May 1920, p. 1.

[8] Halperin, *The Political World of American Zionism,* pp. 259-61.

[9] *The New Palestine,* 7 November 1930, pp. 123-32, 139; *New York Times,* 1 October 1945, p. 1; 2 October 1945, pp. 2-3; 9 October 1945, p. 5; *The New Palestine,* 31 October 1945, pp. 1-2; 12 July 1946, p. 8; *American Jewish Year Book* 48 (1946-1947), pp. 236-37.

[10] Abraham G. Duker, "Emerging Culture Patterns in American Jewish Life," *Publications of the American Jewish Historical Society* 39 (September 1949), p. 371. *Der Tog,* 17 April 1938, p. 2; 18 April 1938, p. 1; 28 April 1940, p. 2; 29 April 1940, p. 1. Interview with David Breslau, Jerusalem, 8 August 1997, and with William Z. Goldfarb, Tel Aviv, 12 August 1997.

[11] *The Maccabaean,* 30:1 (January 1917), p. 144; Hillel Tryster, *Israel Before Israel: Silent Cinema in the Holy Land* (Jerusalem: Steven Spielberg Jewish Film Archive, 1995), p. 21.

[12] *The New Palestine,* 28 October 1932, p. 10; 25 November 1932, p. 6; 23 December 1932, p. 10; 11 December 1933, p. 5; 29 December 1933, p. 8.

[13] Meyer Weisgal, *Meyer Weisgal . . . So Far: An Autobiography* (New York: Random House, 1971), pp. 106-107.

[14] For the full-page advertisement of the Hanukkah festival, see *Reform Advocate,* 10 December 1932, p. 340; for a brief description of the event, see *ibid.,* 31 December 1932, p. 375.

[15] *Chicago Daily Tribune,* 4 July 1933, pp. 1, 4; Weisgal, *. . . So Far,* pp. 113-16; Atay Citron, "Pageantry and Theater in the Service of Jewish Nationalism in the United States, 1933-1946," Ph.D. diss., New York University, 1989, pp. 37-49, 116-19.

[16] *The New Palestine,* 15 August 1934, p. 1; 14 September 1934, p. 13.

[17] *Ibid.,* 12 November 1937, p. 8; 19 November 1937, p. 6.

[18] *Ibid.,* 12 November 1939, p. 8; 19 November 1939, p. 8.

[19] *New York Times,* 21 November 1935, p. 27; Hillel Tryster, "'The Land of Promise': A Case Study in Zionist Film Propaganda," *Historical Journal of Film, Radio and Television* 15:2 (1995), pp. 187-217; Marilyn Gold Koolik, *Constructive and Destructive Uses of Film as Propaganda: Case Studies from Jewish History,* Max and Irene Engel Levy Memorial Lecture (Cambridge, Mass.: Harvard University Library, 1992), pp. 13-14.

[20] *New York Times,* 21 November 1935, p. 27.

[21] Hillel Tryster, "Anatomy of an Epic Film," *Jerusalem Post Magazine,* 30 October 1992, pp. 16-18; *The New Palestine,* 29 November 1935, p. 16.

[22] *The New Palestine,* 22 November 1935, pp. 1, 6.

[23] Meyer Weisgal, *...So Far,* pp. 149-50, 161-63; *The New Palestine,* 2 June 1939, pp. 1-4.

[24] *The New Palestine,* 16 June 1939, p. 8.

[25] *The New Palestine,* 12 May 1939, p. 8; 19 May 1939, pp. 8-10.

[26] Walter Laqueur, *A History of Zionism* (New York: Schocken, 1972), pp. 359-78.

[27] Monty Noam Penkower, "In Dramatic Dissent: The Bergson Boys," *American Jewish History,* 70:3 (March 1981), pp. 281-309; Zvi Ganin, *Truman, American Jewry, and Israel, 1945-*

1948 (New York: Holmes & Meier, 1979), pp. 5-6; Judd L. Teller, *Strangers and Natives, The Evolution of the American Jew from 1921 to the Present* (New York: Delacorte Press, 1968), pp. 202-207.

28 Atay Citron, "Pageantry and Theater," pp. 286-303, 311-36; Stephen J. Whitfield, "The Politics of Pageantry, 1936-1946," *American Jewish History* 84:2 (September 1996), pp. 234-44.

29 Citron, "Pageantry and Theater," pp. 383-84.

30 Citron, "Pageantry and Theater," pp. 393-94; Whitfield, "Politics of Pageantry," pp. 245-50.

31 Citron, "Pageantry and Theater," p. 367; *New York Times,* 5 December 1946, p. 39 (Reply of Gay M. Gillette to Judah L. Magnes); Raphael Medoff, "Menahem Begin as George Washington: The Americanizing of the Jewish Revolt Against the British," *American Jewish Archives* 47:2 (Fall/Winter, 1994), pp. 189-91.

32 *New York Times,* 3 December 1946, p. 41 (Open letter from Judah L. Magnes to Eleanor Roosevelt); Whitfield, "Politics of Pageantry," pp. 249-50.

33 Aviva Halamish, "American Volunteers in Illegal Immigration to Palestine, 1946-1948," *Jewish History* 9:1 (Spring 1995), pp. 91-106.

34 *New York Herald Tribune,* 15 May 1947, p. 17.

35 *PM,* 19 May 1947; "David Breslau, The Story of an Ad," in J.J. Goldberg and Elliot King, eds., *Builders and Dreamers: Habonim Labor Zionist Youth in North America* (New York: Herzl Press, 1993), pp. 95-97; Mazkirut Habonim [Habonim secretariat] to David Ben-Gurion, 24 June 1947, Central Zionist Archives, Jerusalem, Israel. [Marie Syrkin, the Labor Zionist publicist, wrote the text.] For a detailed discussion of the episode, see Yehuda Riemer "How the American Public First Learned about the Haganah," *Shorashim* [Hebrew], 6 (1991), pp. 271-85.

36 *Haganah, Songs of the Jewish Underground* (1947); All recordings mentioned are available in the Jacob Michael collection of Jewish music, National and University Library, Jerusalem. My thanks to Yaacov Mazor for helping to locate them.

37 Pamphlet, "The Chalutzim Series," [1935?], Collection F25, File 330, Central Zionist Archives, Jerusalem.

38 Arthur A. Goren, "'Anu banu artza' in America: The Americanization of the *Halutz* Ideal," in Allon Gal, ed., *Envisioning Israel: Changing Ideals and Images of North American Jews* (Detroit and Jerusalem: Wayne State University Press and Magnes Press, Hebrew University, 1996), pp. 96-98, 102-103.

39 Bracha Zefira, *Kolot Rabim* [Many Voices], (Tel Aviv: Masada, 1978), passim; *Jewish Frontier* 5:6 (June 1938), p. 24; *The New Palestine,* 28 October 1938, p. 6; Corinne Chochem, "Artists in Search of Their People," *The Reconstructionist,* 12:20 (February 1947): pp. 21-23.

40 Nurit Shiloh-Cohen, ed., *The Bezalel of Schatz* (Jerusalem: Israel Museum, 1983), pp. 82-94, 308; *The New Palestine,* 10-17 August 1928, p. 112; 7 December 1928, pp. 467-69.

A Place in the World: Jews and the Holy Land at World's Fairs
by Barbara Kirshenblatt-Gimblett

To be seen or not to be seen—this was the question for Jews participating in world's fairs, from their inception at London's Crystal Palace in 1851 to the establishment of the State of Israel. There were dangers in being shown and risks in being seen. World's fairs were organized along national, imperial, and colonial lines, an arrangement that provided no formal rubric for a diaspora to represent itself as such. Jews turned up just about everywhere at the fairs, just as they did in the world, though in the nineteenth-century fairs, they were generally not visible as Jews, except where religion and race were concerned. Whatever the dangers of being shown and seen, there were also opportunities. Jews used the fairs to set the record straight. They also used the occasion to model themselves, even as they were modeled by others.

At world's fairs in the United States during the nineteenth century, Christians cooperated with their American Jewish contemporaries, but identified Judaism and the Jewish people with a distant place and time—the Holy Land and the world of the Bible. Christians shared the podium with Jews at religion congresses held at the 1893 World's Columbian Exposition in Chicago, praised the contributions of Jews and Judaism to civilization, and collaborated with prominent Jewish citizens on ambitious Holy Land exhibits. Despite their ecumenical spirit, however, Christians represented Jews as an immutable race, stubborn religion, and failed nation, and accorded them a central role within a providential narrative of deicide and restoration. The scene of this story was the Holy Land.

Jewish delegates and exhibitors respectfully insisted that they were American by citizenship and Jewish by religion. They protested that Judaism itself had evolved into a modern religion with universal values and that Jews themselves were modern people in a modern world. Those who dissociated Jews and Judaism from the Land of Israel insisted that "the day of national religions is past."[1] It was heresy to characterize Judaism as a "tribal religion" and Jews as a race.[2]

Nonetheless, two places—the Holy Land of the Bible and the Orient of the Arabian Nights—occupied one space in the minds of visitors to the Chicago fair. Jews were central to both, even if they were only intermittently visible in each. As a cartoon lampooning opportunistic entrepreneurs at the fair suggests, Holy Land and Orient were interchangeable.[3] Captioned "Human Natur'," this cartoon offers the following scenario. "Life in the Holy Lands! Scenes from Biblical Days!!! The Historic East as It Is and Was!!! A Moral Show!!!" When not a single spectator came to this display, the Turkish proprietor changed the sign to "Life in the Harem!! Dreamy Scenes in the Orient!!! Eastern Dances!!! The Sultan's Diversions." To his delight, Christian preachers and Sunday-school teachers now rushed to buy tickets. While the cartoon identifies "Human Natur'" with pious Christian visitors, it does not reveal that the proprietor in the doorway and belly dancer on the placard were in all likelihood Jews, for reasons to be discussed.

The interchangeability of the infidel's delights and the world of Jesus is emblematic of the positional maneuvers that determined the place of Jews in such displays.[4] World's fairs demanded a logical classification of subjects and their clear arrangement in space. The space of display is never neutral. Where,

Barbara Kirshenblatt-Gimblett is Professor of Performance Studies and Professor of Hebrew and Judaic Studies at New York University. Her most recent book, *Destination Culture: Tourism, Museums, and Heritage,* will be published by the University of California Press in 1998. She is currently working on a book entitled *Exhibiting Jews.*

"Human Natur'"
World's Fair Puck, 4 September 1893

for example, would the Jerusalem Exhibit appear at the 1904 Louisiana Purchase Exposition in St. Louis—on the Pike, the amusement strip, or by itself in the very center of the main fairgrounds? Would the Jewish Palestine Pavilion at the 1939 New York World's Fair be on the avenue of national pavilions or in the area dedicated to religious and community groups?

While the position of Jews in these displays was flexible, it was almost invariably inferior, thanks to a conceptual separation between religion and race that produced the following alignments. Whereas Jews shared religion but not race with Christians, they shared race but not religion with Arabs. In displays of "Life in the Holy Land," Christians and Jews shared a religious history—i.e., the Judeo-Christian tradition—that set them apart from Islam. Displays of "Life in the Harem," however, were based on the racial distinction between Aryans (Christians of European origin) versus Semites (Jews and Arabs). Thus, Jews were often present but not visible as Jews in the Oriental displays, whereas they were either absent or an icon of abjection in recreations of "Life in the Holy Land."

Though Jews could be found in the Holy Land itself, many who lived there at the turn of the century had moved to Palestine from various places in the diaspora. Even those who had been there from many generations bore little resemblance to the ancient Israelites imagined by the exhibitors. Though Jews had held steadfast to ancient religious practices and had witnessed the world of Jesus, they had scattered

Palestine display, A Century of Progress
Chicago, 1934
By the 1930s, world's fairs were used to promote Holy Land tourism as well as consumer goods
produced by Jewish settlers in Palestine.

Central Zionist Archives

to the ends of the earth. Exhibitors assumed that Bedouins, not Jews, had preserved the pastoral way of life associated with the Bible and done so in the land of the Bible. Accordingly, Bedouins were thought to offer a better basis than Jews for recreating daily life in the Bible, particularly since such displays had to mediate between the ancient way of life they reconstructed and the present conditions that visitors to the Holy Land actually experienced. Bedouins, considered as living archeology, closed the gap between past and present. Even Jews accepted this

idea. At their fundraising bazaar and fair in New York City in 1916, the People's Relief Committee for the Jewish War Sufferers promoted a "Palestine exhibit" in the form of a Bedouin village, with 150 people in costume: "See and show your children how our ancestors lived in Biblical Times."[5]

By the 1904 St. Louis fair, the Holy Land and Oriental village had become one and the same, as hundreds of Jerusalem natives recreated daily life in a reconstruction of the Old City. Jews could be seen wailing at the Western Wall, an emblematic scene invoking both the Jewish messianic narrative—extending from the destruction of the Second Temple to the coming of the Messiah and restoration of Israel—and the Christian narrative, from the crucifixion of Jesus to the Second Coming. When Jews were not caught in the sleep of providential time at the Wailing Wall, they occupied the Dreamland of Oriental enchantment in the Streets of Constantinople and Cairo, which had become fixtures of the fairs.

Jews also found occasions to control how they positioned and defined themselves at the fairs. Pioneering Semitic scholar Cyrus Adler created exhibitions for the Smithsonian Institution, displaying Bible lands and Bible peoples, which projected his conceptualization of the ancient Near East out to the diaspora and up to the present. He and others disentangled religion from race and nationality and insisted that Judaism was a modern and universalistic religion. Adler's exhibits of the history of world religions positioned Judaism at the beginning of a great story. However, not until the Palestine pavilions of the 1930s would the official Jewish presence at the fair reach out to a world of the future to offer a *model for* a Jewish homeland rather than a *model of* a distant place.[6] The project of establishing a Jewish homeland in Palestine finally placed the Jewish presence at the very heart of the fairs' classification system, namely with other sovereign states.

A Museum of Faiths

Recognizing the agency of display, Jews found ways to negotiate the possibilities and dangers of visibility on a world stage. A grand opportunity presented itself at the 1893 Chicago world's fair, which featured a monumental Parliament of Religions. This gesture of ecumenism, in the spirit of "universal religion," required not only that representatives of the world's religions be present on the dais and speak on behalf of their own faiths. It was also necessary to persuade representatives of the main denominations in the United States (Protestant, Catholic, Jewish) to join the organizing committee, lend their names, endorse the cause, and rally support among their own ranks. How did Jews respond?

Dr. Emil G. Hirsch, leader of the Jewish contingent at the Parliament of Religions, tried to distance Jews from their association with the Holy Land of antiquity and the exotic East of his own time as part of a larger effort to disentangle religion from race and nationality. For the Reform Jews of Chicago, who played such an important role in organizing the denominational congresses at the Chicago fair, the cartoon "Human Natur'" exemplified their worst fears. Jews, they insisted, were not relics of Biblical antiquity, but modern exponents of a universal religion and loyal citizens of the countries in which they lived. They were not immobilized witnesses to Jesus and his world, but part of an evolving history. Nor did Jews form "a distinct nationality or race" or show a "desire to return to Palestine and resurrect the ancient nationality." Jews were "merely an independent religious community."[7] This had been the message at the 1876 Centennial Exhibition in Philadelphia, where the Independent Order B'nai B'rith presented an allegorical statue, "Religious Liberty," by Sir Moses Ezekiel, which made no reference whatsoever to Jews. It was in this spirit that Rabbi Hirsch laid out the elements of universal religion: "the day of national religions is past," he declared, adding that "race and nationality cannot circumscribe the fellowship of the faithful."[8]

Deliberating about how to participate in the fair, Chicago Jews saw a chance to set the record straight: "no religion has been more thoroughly misunderstood and misinterpreted.... Since the existence of our religion, no such opportunity as this has ever been extended to the Jew to set himself right before the whole world. It would, therefore, be criminal negligence did we not embrace this chance to proclaim," through the most credible spokespersons, what Judaism is really about, its contributions to humanity, and its attitudes to other religions.[9] At the same time, even the *Reform Advocate*, which encouraged Jewish involvement in the fair, struck a cautionary note: "We have no doubt, our congresses will be among the best attended by—non-Jews. For, there is no use denying it, for many thousands and thousands of non-Jews, we are a curiosity, a freak, an archeological specimen." This is one reason (indifference being another), the article continues, that "Our own coreligionists will be less eager to assist," for they have an "aversion against being paraded as a 'dime museum freak.'"[10] Their fears were not unfounded.

The Parliament of Religions was to be a "museum of faiths." Delegates, by their very presence, were to create a massive display of the world's faiths. Each religion would stand alone "in its own perfect integrity, uncompromised, in any degree, by its relation to any other," so as to "unite all Religion against all irreligion," the larger purpose of the Parliament.[11] However, speakers who took it upon themselves to talk about Jews and Judaism, well-intended as they were, revealed the extent to which the entire event had been orchestrated to serve the aims of its largely Protestant organizers. They needed to reassure their conservative coreligionists that, in the final analysis, Christianity would not be thought of "as on the same level with other religions" and the whole event itself would exhibit an overtly Christian character. The Lord's Prayer was the only prayer recited each day at the site, and Jews were claimed as Old Testament Christians by John Henry Barrows, Chairman of the General Committee, in his welcoming remarks.[12] In a spirit of reciprocity, he declared his willingness to "call myself a New Testament Jew."[13]

Participants in the Parliament of Religions talked at cross-purposes. Professor D.G. Lyon of Harvard University insisted on using "the word 'Jew' not in the religious but in the ethnic sense" and claimed that, however much they may be citizens of the lands of their birth, Jews "cannot avoid being known as the scattered fragments of a nation. Most of them

are as distinctly marked by mental traits and by physiognomy as is a typical Englishman, German, or Chinaman."[14] Rabbi Joseph Silverman of Temple Emanu-El in New York protested that "Jew is not to be used parallel with German, Englishman, American, but with Christian, Catholic, Protestant" and other faiths, anticipating what would become the interfaith movement several decades later.[15] But to no avail. Religion quickly became a matter of nationality and nationality a question of race. All three were anchored in the Holy Land, home of the Semites.

It was the Indian theist P.C. Mozoomar, of Calcutta, however, who most clearly mapped the fateful contrast between Aryan and Semite, which identified Christians with Indo-European dynamism and Jews with Oriental immobility.[16] While Christians and Jews were linked historically through religion, the designations Aryan and Semite provided them with separate racial and linguistic genealogies, geographies, and historical capacities. Aryans, who emanated from India, evolved, while Semites, who originated in the Near East, did not: in the words of Mozoomar, "The Hebrews, the chosen of Jehovah, with their long line of law and prophets, how are they? Wanderers on the face of the globe, driven by king and kaiser; the objects of persecution to the cruel or objects of sympathy to the kind. Mount Moriah is in the hands of the Mussulman, Zion is silent, and over the ruins of Solomon's Temple a few men beat their breasts and wet their white beards with their tears."[17] Could today's Jews live up to the glorious past of "the little nation of Palestine," Professor Lyon asked.[18] No wonder Rabbi Silverman complained that "The evolution which Judaism has undergone in the past two thousand years, seems to be an unknown quantity in the minds of many."[19]

Rather than identifying Jews with the Holy Land, Rabbi David Philipson associated them with the founding of the United States. Declaring that the Puritans founded America on the basis of the

Old Testament and modeled it on the old Jewish state, he appealed to Protestant visions of America as the new Jerusalem. Professor Lyon agreed: "A Jewish empire does not exist, and Jerusalem is not the mistress of the world. And yet the dream of the prophet is true. A home for the oppressed has been found, a home where prosperity and brotherhood dwell together. Substitute America for Jerusalem and a republic for a kingdom, and the correctness of the prophet's dream is realized."[20] It is this identification of America as the new Zion that defined Christians' interest in the Holy Land itself, their view of Jews as a Bible people, and the appeal of exhibitions dealing with the lands and peoples of the Bible.

An Exhibition of Religion

Contrary to the Parliament of Religions, which insisted that believers speak on behalf of their faiths and avoid comparison, Cyrus Adler and Morris Jastrow, who taught Semitics and Assyriology at the University of Pennsylvania, argued that the scientific study of religion required comparative and historical perspectives independent of faith.[21] They upheld three principles: a religion should be presented from the perspective of its adherents, though not necessarily by its adherents; all religions must be treated with respect; and displays should focus on underlying religious ideas, not church history or doctrinal disagreements. Such displays would help foster religion as a field of scientific study and, through it, promote religious tolerance.

Adler encouraged the participants in the Parliament of Religions to attend three religion exhibitions at the fair—his own on the history of religion in the Government Building, a second one on the religion of "primitive" peoples in the Anthropology Building, and the Turkish mosque on the Midway Plaisance. Had they visited the Turkish mosque on September 19, 1893, they would have heard Kol Nidre recited by Jews "from all parts of the Orient,"

including not only Constantinople, but also Adrianople, Tunis, Tripoli, Damascus, Smyrna, Bombay, Calcutta, Algeria, and other places, for reasons to be discussed below.[22]

Adler's exhibition, which made his programmatic statements concrete, differed in important ways from the other religion exhibitions he listed. First, he refused to allow Jews as well as Judaism, Christianity, and other world religions to be compared with "primitive" religions. Second, he would not allow the adherents of these religions to be incorporated into anthropology's racial typologies and evolutionary sequences and modes of display—models in plaster of heads, wax mannequins in national dress, and artifacts arranged to show progress in development from the simple to the complex. Not surprisingly, Adler's exhibition on the history of religions was located in the Government Building, not in the Anthropology Building, even though the sections that Adler directed at the Smithsonian were part of the Department of Anthropology.[23]

Instead, Adler limited his exhibit "to a selection from the religions of the nations inhabiting the Mediterranean basin, with special regard to the ceremonies as forming the starting point for a comparative study of religions. The exhibit comprises the following religions: Assyro-Babylonian, Jewish, Mohammedan, Greek, Roman and Oriental Christian," the official catalogue of the United States Government Building explained.[24] Moreover, he located Judaism not in relation to the Holy Land, but within the much wider Mediterranean basin. Adler removed Judaism from a Christian geography and teleology and placed it strategically within a broader religious arena.

At the same time, by treating "religion as a distinct subject" and making each religion the basic unit of exhibition, Adler rejected a geographical or national approach. The integrity of a religion would be lost if exhibits were divided up according to the many countries in which one religion was found. Accordingly, Adler deemphasized the historical and regional particularities of the objects and the communities from which they came in order to pursue a normative treatment of cult and creed. Adler's approach was consistent with a more general policy of the U.S. National Museum, as the Smithsonian's National Museum of Natural History was then known, which treated "special subjects independently of areas or national limitations in order to show the history of given ideas or endeavors in the human race treated as an entity."[25] The heterogeneity of the United States as a nation of immigrants may have added to the appeal of such integrative arrangements for the organizers, if not for immigrant visitors.

Interestingly, the only exhibit of Jewish interest mentioned in the Yiddish guide to the 1893 World's Columbian Exposition was the treasures sent by the Pope from the Vatican, among which were gold and silver utensils that Titus is alleged to have taken from the Temple in Jerusalem.[26] The Yiddish guide assumed its immigrant readers would be more interested in exhibits of the latest goods and machines, or in seeing how various states treat their citizens, make coins, deal with foreigners, and handle immigrants: "One can see how emigrants are received in America" in the Foreign Ministry display in the United States Government Building, the guide noted.[27] This guide did not tell them that in the same building could be found an exhibition on the history of religion with Judaism at its center. Nor did the guide mention Jewish participation in the Parliament of Religions and denominational congresses.

Although Adler's exhibit attracted little notice in the press, the *New York Evening Post* did review it in detail, noting that the collection was paralleled only by the holdings of the Royal Museum in Berlin.[28] Adler succeeded in using this exhibition to secure from the U.S. National Museum a commitment to foster the comparative study of religion, establish a new Section of Religious Ceremonials dedicated to this field, and ensure that Judaica would be well represented in the collection. As Grace Cohen Grossman notes, "The first major group of objects of Judaica acquired by the Smithsonian were those obtained specifically for the World's Columbian Exposition."[29]

People of Bible Lands

In Adler's exhibitions, the Holy Land was supplanted not only by the Mediterranean Basin, but also by an even wider concept of "Bible peoples." Adler's exhibitions located the origins of Western civilization in this region and positioned Judaism and Jews strategically within that history. In his exhibitions of *religious ceremonials,* Judaism inaugurated the great Judeo-Christian tradition. In his exhibitions of *Biblical antiquities,* Jews were a "Bible people."

Adler's exhibitions of Biblical antiquities for the U.S. National Museum were displayed at world's fairs in Cincinnati (1888), Atlanta (1895), and Tennessee (1897). They featured material from what had started out as the Oriental Antiquities section—this section, whose establishment was initiated in 1887, was formed partly at Adler's urging.[30] For practical reasons, the Oriental Antiquities section was dedicated to "Biblical archeology—to the history, archeology, languages, arts and religions of the peoples of Western Asia and Egypt," with an emphasis on illustrating Biblical history.[31]

A key to Adler's success was the emerging field of Semitic studies. Adler was the first person to receive a Ph.D. in Semitics from an American university (Johns Hopkins). Semitic studies brought the disciplines of archaeology, ethnology, paleography, philology, and the history of religion to bear on the peoples and civilizations of the Mediterranean. This field was particularly congenial to Jewish scholars in America. First, while it included the study of the Bible, its scope was much broader. Second, Semitic studies offered a relatively safe context for Jews pursuing Bible studies, because it required rigorous scholarship unencumbered by sectarian loyalties and theological issues. Third, Semitic studies positioned Jews advantageously in the history of civilization, and by extension, enhanced their standing in Adler's own day.

According to Adler, Biblical archeology encompassed the "language, history, social life, arts, and religion of the Biblical nationalities."[32] Through three conceptual leaps, Adler made Biblical science encompass 5,000 years of history and the entire Mediterranean region, from Western Asia to Egypt, including not only its ancient inhabitants, but also their modern descendants, among them European Jewry. He argued, first that, "Owing to the intense conservatism of oriental peoples, a careful study of the modern inhabitants of western Asia may exhibit in a new aspect the manners and customs of former times."[33] Living evidence supporting this theory was exhibited in foreign villages on the Midway Plaisance.

"Nor is the area covered less extensive than the period of time," he continued. "Roughly speaking, it would require that one point of a compass be placed in Jerusalem, and a radius of a thousand miles be selected to describe a circle which would include all of the people with whom the Israelites came into contact during their national existence."[34] The historical and geographical parameters of Biblical sci-

Costume display, Harvard University Semitic Museum
Cambridge, Mass., 1903
Artifacts of contemporary life in Palestine, such as these garments acquired from turn-of-the-century Jews and Bedouins, were frequently displayed at world's fairs and in museum exhibitions to represent the "unchanging" culture of Bible lands.

Semitic Museum, Harvard University

ence were thus defined in terms of the ancient Israelites—their center in Jerusalem, their range of contacts, and the persistence of their practices among other peoples today. Bedouins, for example, were presumed to have preserved a Biblical way of life: many objects currently in use in Palestine and surrounding lands "differ in no wise from those used in ancient times" and are, "it may be assumed, in the 'unchanging East' essentially the same at the present day as in Bible times."[35] Thus, Adler's exhibits could feature flutes recently made by Bedouins and a "modern Egyptian brick from Thebes."[36] Finally, Adler made it possible to include in Biblical science virtually anything from the Jewish diaspora that could be shown to fulfill a Biblical precept. This, for example, was the rationale for exhibiting an eighteenth-century German Sabbath lamp.

The practical outcome of these conceptual leaps was a more impressive exhibition. Once Adler was able to consolidate collections otherwise divided between religious ceremonials and oriental antiquities, he had more objects to work with.[37] A comprehensive *Biblical Antiquities* exhibition at the 1895 Cotton States International Exposition in Atlanta included geology (dust from Jerusalem and water from the Jordan), flora and fauna, birds, reptiles, and insects; Palestinian antiquities (mainly casts); recently made musical instruments; precious stones of Palestine, "with a model illustrating the method in which the gems were placed in the high priest's breastplate"; coins of Bible lands; dress, ornaments, and household utensils; Jewish religious ceremonials; antiquities (Egypt, Assyria and Babylonia, Hittites); and a collection of Bibles, including ancient versions and modern translations.[38] The exhibition also featured several models—an Egyptian mummy and a temple tower of Babylon, based on Herodotus and recent reports on the ruin.

Jews were not the target audience for this and other exhibits of Biblical archeology or Biblical science, as Adler preferred to call this field, in recognition of the living material it included. The exhibit was a response to "the wide-spread interest in biblical studies" and intended to "enable Bible students (of whom it is estimated that there are already more than four millions in the Sunday-schools of the United States)" to enhance their study of the text by seeing how specialists study "the people of Bible lands" and examining the archeological material, photographs, casts, inscriptions, and artifacts on display.[39]

Given the debates over whether Jews were a people, nation, race, or religion, Adler had found an ingenious way to present Judaism as a unified religion, and by implication, Jews as a unified religious community, while "denationalizing" religion. Drawing on Semitic studies as a framework, Adler could stress commonalities among the peoples of Bible lands and avoid exclusivity in the treatment of Judaism. Moreover, as Adler made explicit in his speech at the formal opening of the Harvard University Semitic Museum in 1903, "It is coming to be more and more recognized that in everything which makes for the higher life the modern man derived directly from a few groups of people that lived about the Mediterranean, and that knowledge of their civilization is essential to an understanding of the higher history of human thought."[40] The slightly defensive tone of this affirmation indexes current debates over

whether Western civilization derived from Semitic or Aryan sources.

"Life in the Harem"

This debate informed the live displays in foreign villages and souvenir portrait albums based on them. The original plan for these villages at the Chicago fair was to arrange them so as to show the evolution of humankind from Africa (as represented by the Dahomeans) to Europe (the Irish, Germans, Austrians, and Dutch), with the Near East (Turkey, Egypt, Algeria, Tunisia) and Far East (Java, Japan) arrayed between them. Practical considerations precluded so tidy an arrangement. Needless to say there was no Jewish village. What would it have been? The Jewish immigrant quarter in Chicago?

Yet, Jews were ubiquitous on the Midway, though invisible, with telling exceptions:

> About four-fifths of the inhabitants of the Turkish village on the Midway Plaisance at the Chicago Exposition were Jews. Merchants, clerks, actors, servants, musicians, and even the dancing girls, were of the Mosaic faith, though their looks and garb would lead one to believe them Mohammedans. That their Judaism was not of the passive character was demonstrated by the closed booths, shops, and curio places, by the silence in the otherwise noisy theaters and the general Sabbath day air which pervaded the "Streets of Constantinople" on Yom Kippur—the Day of Atonement.[41]

In other words, they were conspicuous by their absence.

While the cartoon "Human Natur'" establishes the interchangeability of the Oriental village and the Holy Land, it does not indicate the centrality of Jews to each type of display at the fair. In the cartoon, the proprietor and belly dancer are Turkish and presumed to be Moslem, while the visitors they attract are Christian preachers and Sunday-school teachers. As it turns out, however, Jews managed not only particular concessions, but also the Midway as a whole. Frederic Ward Putnam, a Harvard anthropologist, was originally put in charge of the Midway, but he was replaced by Sol Bloom, as it became clear that the Midway was more show business than ethnology. Born in the Midwest of Polish-Jewish parents and raised in San Francisco, Bloom had been so impressed with the Algerian village at the Paris world's fair in 1889, that at the end of that fair he arranged to have exclusive rights to presenting the village in the United States. Bloom found the perfect opportunity to do so at the Chicago fair.[42]

The Turkish village was the largest one on the Midway. Some eighty percent of the hundreds of people working there were Jewish, as were some of the most celebrated "Oriental dancers" on the Midway— among them Nazha Kassik, "a native of Beyrouth, Syria," and Rahlo Jammele, "a native of Jerusalem," both of whom performed in the Moorish palace among other places on the Midway.[43] In a word, many of the "Sultan's Diversions" announced in the *Puck* cartoon were performed by

Portrait of Rahlo Jammele, "Jewish Dancing Girl"
Portrait Types of the Midway Plaisance,
World's Fair Art Series (St. Louis: N.D. Thompson, 1894)
One of a series of portraits of racial "types" on view at the 1893 Chicago fair. The original caption reads, in part: "She is a native of Jerusalem, where she early learned the dances of that country; and while still a child she was instructed in the ancient dances of the peculiar people. Her sword dance had in it much that was startling and not a little that was amusing, and never failed to win for the fair performer a generous round of applause."

Collection of Barbara Kirshenblatt-Gimblett

Jews—in their capacity as Orientals.

The large number of Jews working on the Midway was due in no small measure to Cyrus Adler, who was appointed Commissioner of the World's Columbian Exposition to Turkey, Palestine, Persia, Egypt, Tunis, and Morocco.[44] Palestine was under the control of the Sultan in Constantinople, who did not accord it much political importance. However, Jerusalem was a large and important administrative unit extending well beyond the city itself, and Jews were the largest population within the city proper during the mid-nineteenth century. While performers from Palestine did appear at the Chicago fair, it was not in a Palestine village but on a recreated street of Constantinople. Thus, Palestine was subsumed under Turkey.

While Adler did not propose a Jewish village for the Midway Plaisance, he did give concessions to Jewish dragomen (translators and guides), who were experienced at explaining their region to strangers. Dragomen also assisted entrepreneurs in the business of tourism, which was sometimes combined with international trade. In the case of the Turkish display, "A Constantinople Street Scene," Adler gave the concession to Souhami, Sadhullah and Co., whom he characterized as "the largest merchants in the Constantinople bazaar."[45] Robert Levy was married to one of the partners in this company, an American woman who was related to a family that Adler knew in Baltimore. Levy became the manager and chief proprietor of the Turkish village, as well as manager of the personnel in the Near East exhibits on the Midway.

By some estimates, Levy brought more than 200 people to live and work in the Turkish village; the preponderance of Jews among them would seem to be supported by complaints from visitors. According to Denton J. Snider, who was there, "Some have said that all this does not represent Turkey, and that the Turkish village is purely a speculative enterprise of some Oriental Jews," though he did concede that "the originators, whoever they may be, are seeking to represent Turkey . . . and have given the village a distinctive Turkish meaning."[46] Levy supplemented his Turkish contingent with "young American men and women to perform diverse chores within the Turkish village . . . as maids and cashiers in the soft-drink pavilion."[47] A controversy erupted when they refused to wear "Oriental costumes...including gorgeous bloomers." They objected to "bifurcated garments," even in the interest of "realism," an objection that was part of a larger debate at the fair over dress reform.[48]

There was at least one point, however, where it was deemed important to distinguish these Jews *as Jews,* and that was in the photographic portraits of "individual types of various nations from all parts of the world who represented, in the Department of Ethnology, the manners, customs, dress, religions, music and other distinctive traits and peculiarities of their Race."[49] Here, in book form, Putnam finally succeeded in creating the panorama of the world's races that he had hoped to realize on the Midway. It is here that Jews, and in particular Jews in the Turkish and Egyptian villages, appeared as a racial type and specifically as Semites. These portraits are an extension of the photo-identifications that controlled the entry of thousands of fair workers and officials.[50] Indeed, many of them were made by the same photographer.[51]

The three most accepted ways to represent racial types were first, to select a person considered typical of the race, and to photograph the head, which was considered the most important indicator of racial type. This method was considered the least scientific. Second, anthropologists such as Franz Boas applied the methods of Alphonse Bertillon, who used measurements, standardized images, and a special filing system to facilitate identification of particular criminals (and victims), as well as social and criminal types. Third, Francis Galton in London and Dr. Dudley Sargent in the United States used the composite method. Galton superimposed images of members of a race to establish the type, while Sargent worked from photographs of naked freshman at Harvard and Radcliffe, as well as measurement statistics, to arrive at the body form of "the typical college male and female" as shown in "anthropometric statues." Deviations from the norm were to be corrected by appropriate training and exercise. These materials were on view in the most popular section of the Anthropology Building, where Boas and psychologist Joseph Jastrow, both of them Jews, assisted Frederic Ward Putnam, the director of anthropological exhibits for the entire fair. For a small fee, visitors could be examined, measured, and compared to standard types.[52]

Bertillon's systematic filing system for hundreds of thousands of photographs put the body in the archive, while the composite portraits made by Galton and Sargent put the archive in the body, to invoke Alan Sekula's distinction.[53] The corporal archive offered yet another basis for identifying Jews with the Holy Land long after their dispersal. As the caption for "Rebecca Meise Alithensii (Jewess)" explains:

Though the Jews are no longer a nation and

properly claim citizenship in all countries, there is no racial type that has been so persistent through many centuries and amid such varied environment. Whether in Palestine or America, in the Tenth Century before or the Nineteenth Century after Christ, the Jew shows the same physical characteristics, slightly modified by his surroundings, and the same intellectual acumen and business capacity that have made him the most successful financier in the world. This handsome oriental lady was born of Jewish parents in Constantinople twenty-seven years ago; and, while retaining evidences of her blood, she is in general appearance a fair type of Turkish beauty, and her dress gives an exact idea of the picturesque and gorgeous costume of that nation....[54]

The racial type had to be derived from an individual portrait, and it was the burden of the caption to make a persuasive case for the attribution. The assumption, certainly on the part of visitors, was that pure racial types would be found in foreign villages devoted exclusively to a single type, and that Jews were the purest race of all.

However, as the caption for a group portrait of Monahan Levi, Isaac Cohn, and H. Hondon explained, no such perfect fit between type and scene had been achieved:

The Turkish village, like many another village on the Midway which was primarily intended to depict certain national characteristics and peculiarities, contained within its walls a good many things which were by no means Turkish, and which are seldom, if ever, found in a genuine Turkish village but may be seen in Constantinople, which is one of the most cosmopolitan cities of the world. Here might be found at times Egyptians, Turks, Jews, Greeks, Syrians, Armenians and representatives of nearly all the nations bordering on the Mediterranean and the countries east thereof.[55]

On the Midway, Rachel Meise Alithensii and the three men in the group portrait signified Turkey. In the souvenir album, however, they were marked as Jews. Yet, even Adler had been unable to tell who was Jewish when he was in Turkey: "When I first began to walk around Constantinople and the villages I could not distinguish the populations at all....The Jews did not have any distinguishing characteristics."[56]

This difficulty in no way restrained the claims made for Jewish racial purity and for "Oriental" Jews as the purest examples of the Jewish racial type. Consider the caption for Far-Away-Moses:

The Jews are the most remarkable of all races. No other people can boast a lineage so ancient and so unbroken. The historian Freeman says: "They are very nearly, if not absolutely, a pure race in a sense in which no other race is pure." Their early history constitutes a body of sacred writings which, considered as literature alone, stands unequalled.... The above portrait is another illustration of the persistence of the Jewish type. This man, who rejoices in the expressive sobriquet of Far-Away-Moses, is the descendant of Jews who were driven from Spain by Queen Isabella. He is fifty-five years old and resides in Constantinople. He speaks many languages and is a noted dragoman. He has been immortalized by Mark Twain, whom he had the honor of conducting through the Holy Land.[57]

Far-Away-Moses, as it turns out, was one of the

partners in the company that held the concession for the Turkish village—he was none other than Harry R. Mandil, one of the two American partners.[58] He was also the model for the Semite head in the ethnological series of thirty-three races that adorn the keystones above the windows on the first floor of the Library of Congress.[59] Had Mandil appeared clean shaven in a business suit as an American citizen, would he have been chosen as the model for the Semite head?

On the Midway, Jews came into focus as Jews only when the camera attempted to fix and arrange racial types in the abstract space of the album. On the ground, they were proxies for others, including Turks, Algerians, and Egyptians. As for the foreign villages themselves, the Mediterranean ones were not only cosmopolitan but also porous, like the regions they represented. Performers moved around the Midway from the Moorish village to the Turkish, Egyptian, and Algerian villages, and back. Captions in various albums identify the same people as Algerians or Turks. Some visitors to the fair expressed anxiety about the "truth" of what they saw, as was the case at earlier European fairs. Not only were immigrants recruited to work in the villages, but American college students also dressed up as natives. As the case of Far-Away-Moses demonstrates, even those who had come from abroad might not be what they seemed.

Jerusalem display, Louisiana Purchase Exposition
St. Louis, Mo., 1904
H.C. White Co.

Library of Congress

"Life in the Holy Lands"

At the Chicago fair, "Life in the Harem" had won out over "Life in the Holy Lands." At the 1904 St. Louis fair, organizers hoped to combine the best of both types of exhibitions in a grand reconstruction of the Old City of Jerusalem. They would create an immersive environment where tourist-pilgrims could identify with what they saw. However fascinating the streets of Cairo and Constantinople or the Dahomean and Javanese villages, visitors to the Chicago fair had approached them with a mixture of fascination and disdain. They alternated between prurient interest and distanced observation. The "ethnographic" character of such displays was often a pretext for licentious performances. On the Midway Plaisance at the Chicago fair, the Persian theater was closed down briefly because the dances were so provocative. The Moorish Palace, one of several contexts in which Jewish dancers performed, was more funhouse than museum. The St. Louis fair's Jerusalem Exhibit would combine the appeal of such immersive environments with the protocols of pilgrimage and religiously motivated tourism in a largely Protestant mode.

However inclusive their claims, the organizers of the Jerusalem Exhibit operated in Christian terms: the Holy Land was associated first and foremost with the life of Jesus and not with Adler's "Bible lands," which extended out from Jerusalem 1,000 miles in all directions and through more than 5,000 years of history. The Jerusalem Exhibit, like Christian tours of the Holy Land, was organized to retrace the steps of Jesus. Indeed, the *Souvenir Album* reproduced images not of the exhibit but of photographs made in the Old City itself, juxtaposed with line drawings of scenes from the Passion thought to have occurred in the locations shown. The images themselves were arranged, for the most part, in the order of the Stations of the Cross and matched with the relevant Biblical passages. The *Souvenir Album* was thus like other commemorative volumes that arranged photographic images of the Holy Land according to the chronology of Jesus' life, whether as a memento of a pilgrimage taken or as a substitute for it.[60] One of the most extensive such volumes was *Earthly Footsteps of the Man of Galilee,* a collection of 400 photographs.[61] Those visiting the St. Louis fair and reading the *Souvenir Album* were "tourist pilgrims" on a sacred itinerary.

Architectural elevation of a model of Temple of Solomon by John Wesley Kelchner, Helme and Corbett Architects New York, 1913
This model was designed to be displayed at the U.S. Sesquicentennial Exposition, held in Philadelphia in 1927.

Center for Judaic Studies, University of Pennsylvania Library

The mode of pilgrimage invoked by the Jerusalem Exhibit was distinctly Protestant. Catholics, who visited shrines dating from at least the Middle Ages, associated pilgrimage with indulgences and pardons and looked to Rome as their headquarters. The Stations of the Cross procession, which can be conducted anywhere, is a medieval innovation brought back to Europe by pilgrims who had visited the Holy Land.[62]

Protestants, who came relatively late to the Holy Land, treated the entire landscape as both shrine and text—it was literally a fifth Gospel.[63] The Bible was their guide book and Jesus, rather than Mary and the saints, their focus. Literal connections between text and place informed not only their travels to the Holy Land, but also their meticulous models, panoramas, and other recreations of it.

Indeed, many Protestant travelers to the Holy Land complained that what they saw was not the place as it was during Jesus' lifetime, but the shrines, churches, and mosques built by Eastern Orthodox, Catholic, and Islamic groups. The challenge for Protestant visitors was to *not* see what was before them. The spectacular religious style of such holy places as the Church of the Holy Sepulcher was antithetical to Protestant austerity. Instead, Protestant pilgrims were more likely to stand in a place and imagine in their mind's eye what they could not see in actuality; to find landscapes that had not yet been touched, as far as they could tell; and to discover through archaeology what the ancient world really looked like.

For these reasons, exhibits of the Holy Land had a distinct advantage over visiting the actual place. The exhibit could achieve a better fit between expectation—and, for that matter, textual and archaeological knowledge—and experience. Distracting and irrelevant elements, particularly those from later periods, could be eliminated. The goal was to make the Biblical text more "real" and the experience of it as vivid and immediate as possible. Paradoxically, the model might achieve this objective better than the Holy Land itself. For Jews, in contrast, the attachment to the Land of Israel was covenantal, and this was the determining factor in identifying holy places, the Wailing Wall chief among them, and creating models, most often of the Tabernacle and the Temple.

While indebted to the foreign villages in the commercial amusement zone of world's fairs, the Jerusalem Exhibit was not located on the Pike, but at the center of the fair grounds proper. It was allotted about ten acres and estimated to require one million dollars. The managers went so far as to declare that "The display will, in short, be Jerusalem itself," if not better; visitors would learn more with less hassle and actually see and understand things inaccessible in Jerusalem itself, where ignorant guides repeat apocryphal tales.[64]

While aiming to combine the enlightenment and uplift of sacred pilgrimage with the amusement of commercial entertainment, the prospectus cautioned that "There is one feature of this display which will be insisted upon by the management, and that is, that it shall be free from anything which will in the least detract from its dignity and solemnity. The features which have been so prominent in so-called Oriental displays exhibited in late years will be conspicuous by their absence. Everything possible will be done to give an educational value to the exhibit."[65] Unlike the Streets of Cairo and Constantinople, Jerusalem "is an unworldly city; it is without a theater, or a barroom or a dance house."[66] Accordingly, Jews would wail at the Wall rather than dance in the café.

Madame Lydia M. von Finkelstein Mountford, a well-known speaker who frequently conducted tours of models of Jerusalem, was to deliver "her wonderful lectures on picturesque Palestine and its people" each day.[67] She claimed to have been born and raised in Jerusalem and would dress up in local costume to give her lectures, a common practice even among lecturers reporting on their travels to Jerusalem on their return home. At Palestine Park, an extensive model of the Holy Land created for the Chautauqua Assembly in Western New York in the 1870s, Protestant visitors dressed up in Oriental dress.[68] Having recreated the landscape and emptied it of people, they now projected themselves into it. If they could not inhabit the Holy Land itself, they could inhabit the model.

While the organizers of the Jerusalem Exhibit assured prospective investors of a good profit on what they expected to be the most popular attraction at the fair, they made no effort to adjust their appeal to Jews for money and endorsements. A form letter simply stated, "It is our intention to present the greatest religious exhibit of modern times, and we are sure that, as a minister of the Gospel, you will be interested in this great enterprise." The letter continued, "in assisting us you will be furthering the cause of Christianity" and making a good financial investment.[69] Nevertheless, Jews did sign on to the project. Three rabbis, Leon Harrison (Temple Israel), Samuel Sale (Shaare Emeth Congregation), and J.H. Messing (United Hebrew Congregation) were members of the Advisory Board. This was not the only aspect of the fair that the Jews of St. Louis supported.

Five prominent St. Louis Jews were appointed to the directorate of the fair, among them Hon. Nathan Frank, a congressman. He used his influence not only to make St. Louis the site of the fair, but also to secure appropriations for the enterprise. Other Jews also raised large sums of money for the fair and served on important committees. Anticipating that Jews, including distinguished scholars from Europe, would come to St. Louis to visit the fair, an article devoted to "The Jews of the World's Fair City: The Part Which They Have Taken in the Upbuilding of St. Louis and the Exposition" promoted both the fair and the "renaissance of Judaism...accompanying the rejuvenescence of St. Louis."[70] It pointed out sites connected with the Jewish community and its institutions. While the prominence of Jews in the organization of the fair was taken as a sign that they were "no longer one of the Children of the Ghetto," the author hastened to add that "the Jew is more or less separate and distinct in his social as in his religious life."[71]

With respect to the fair, the only exhibit this article singled out for description was the one devoted to Jerusalem. Readers were told that the reconstruction of Jerusalem was "an object-lesson for the Biblical student."[72] As for sites within Jerusalem associated with Jews, the highlight was to be "The Jews' Wailing Place," which the fundraising prospectus had described as follows:

> This remarkable spot, which on every Friday afternoon or Saturday morning is frequented by a number of Jews, men and women of all ages and from all countries, pale, deformed and sad, will be reproduced in all its picturesqueness. To the thoughtful, the sight of the Jews who are found there weeping, chanting between penitential sobs portions of the prophetic writings, is a touching and prophetic one; with tears running down their cheeks, kissing the stones, thrusting their faces into the chinks of the wall and fondly resting their heads against it, they acknowledge their sins and the sins of their nation, and beseech the Almighty for pardon and ask that their once holy and beloved House, of which this Wailing Place is part of the western wall, may be quickly rebuilt.[73]

Paradoxically, Jews were not even at home in what was once their homeland. Those at the Wailing Wall were seen as the most abject of all, a shadow of the former glory of ancient Israel. Though all Jews were cursed to wander as a punishment for deicide and their refusal to convert to Christianity, those who stayed in the diaspora were considered better off than those who remained or returned to the Holy Land. As Herman Melville, a Catholic, wrote, in 1856, upon visiting the Holy Land, "In the emptiness of the lifeless antiquity of Jerusalem the emigrant Jews are like flies that have taken up their abode in a skull."[74] American Protestants visiting the Holy Land attributed what they saw to "providential purpose yet to be accomplished."[75] But the Jews on whom they projected the trajectory of Christian destiny bore a very different relationship to the Land of Israel, the Jewish community there, and to world Jewry.

Consistent with the plan to exhibit natives in their native surroundings, the prospectus promised to provide a "Jewish rabbi conducting the ceremonials of his religion in a synagogue which will be a reproduction of the one in which he conducts the worship at Jerusalem."[76] These activities were no mere "imitation ceremony," but "the actual ceremony with their own people in attendance."[77] Hundreds of such natives would march daily in a grand procession and "take a part in the illustrations of Bible life, scenes and customs of the Holy Land for thousands of years."[78]

Moreover, the editor's note on the title page explains: "There are eight Jerusalems lying one upon another. First–City of Jebusites; Second–City of Solomon; Third–City of Nehemia; Fourth–City of Herod destroyed by Titus; Fifth–Emperor Hadrian began to rebuild in the year A.D. 130; Sixth–City of the Early Moslems; Seventh–City of the Crusaders; Eighth–City of the Later Moslems. In A.D. 1244, Jerusalem was besieged for the last time." This history of Jerusalem stops in 1244; its acknowledgment of Jewish presence there ends even earlier, though the captions to the images do refer to more recent events. One would never know from this account that the blue and white Zionist flag was flying at the St. Louis fair.

Anticipating a Jewish State

Meyer Weisgal's Zionist pageant *The Romance of a People* at the 1933 Century of Progress Exposition in Chicago (which extended to 1934) and the Jewish Palestine Pavilion he organized at the 1939 New York World's Fair (which extended to 1940) were radical departures from earlier displays dedicated to the Holy Land or Bible lands at earlier fairs. They were, however, linked to them as well as to Palestine exhibits in British colonial expositions, trade fairs in Palestine, and Palestine pavilions at world's fairs in Paris in the 1930s.

After World War I, the Ottoman Empire fell and in 1920, Palestine came under the British Mandate, after some 400 years of Turkish occupation. Restrictive legislation brought immigration to America to a trickle in 1921 and by 1924, the period of mass immigration was over. With the worldwide depression and the rise of fascism in Europe and anti-Semitism in the United States, relief efforts and pressures to form a Jewish state intensified. In America during the 1930s, Zionism was on the rise across the Jewish spectrum. It is in this context that Weisgal organized his extravagant pageants and ambitious pavilion, ventures that were national and international in scope and explicit in their fundraising, relief, and political goals. Weisgal made brilliant use of performance and exhibition for "propaganda" purposes, the term he used, and political mobilization.[79]

Whereas earlier exhibits were models of something that already or once existed, Weisgal's efforts were dedicated primarily to creating models for what was to come. Weisgal was not the first to create models for a future homeland, but he was the most successful in using pageants and pavilions to mobilize American grass roots support for the Zionist cause. Zionist displays looked to the future. They used the past, understood as deep Jewish roots in the land of the Bible and a subsequent history of

Tapestry with Palestine monuments
Bezalel School of Arts and Crafts, Jerusalem, n.d.
Display of Bezalel crafts at world's fairs and Zionist congresses promoted the work of the school, founded in Jerusalem in 1906, which was dedicated to training Jewish settlers to be skilled artisans and to creating a modern aesthetic for the Zionist movement.

Collection of Bella Lewensohn Schafer

persecution, to add weight to the legitimacy of a future Jewish state in Palestine and its practical necessity. Exhibitions demonstrating the potential and success of agricultural and industrial development there attested to the feasibility of such a state. Palestine exhibits intended to spur trade and investment, as well as Jewish colonization, had appeared since the 1890s, often in connection with Zionist Congresses in Europe and with later British imperial displays. Standard features of such displays were exhibits devoted to the work of the Bezalel School, models of the Tabernacle and Temple, sometimes with guides in costume to explain their features, and stalls showing the success of Jewish efforts in agriculture, manufacture and trade, industry and commerce. An exhibit dedicated to Palestine at the 1933 Chicago fair promoting tourism and trade is a case in point.

The quality of the exhibits themselves became more professional with the advent of the Levant Fairs in Tel Aviv in the 1920s and their blossoming in the '30s. The Levant Fairs not only promoted trade and industry but also showcased the talents of the Levant Fair Studios in the design and fabrication of exhibits. Recognizing the power of display to encourage economic development, the Levant Fair Studios circulated exhibitions promoting Palestine trade and industry through Central and Eastern Europe. By the 1930s, the Levant Fair Studios were producing exhibits for Palestine pavilions at fairs in Paris (1931, 1937) and other European cities, as well as in New York (1939-1940). These exhibits were to be about Palestine right down to their very fabrication; this point was stressed both in official fair publications and by exhibiting a glass model of the Levant Fair itself within the Jewish Palestine Pavilion at the 1939 New York World's Fair.

During the early 1930s, when he was looking for a powerful way to mobilize support for the Zionist cause, Weisgal rejected the idea of a building or exhibit, choosing instead a pageant. A few years later, when

Jewish Palestine Pavilion, World's Fair
New York, 1939

Hadassah, The Women's Zionist Organization of America

Henry Montor, chief fundraiser for the United Palestine Appeal, approached him about Jewish participation in the New York World's Fair of 1939, Weisgal toyed with the idea of a pageant.[80] It was, however, his proposal for a Palestine Pavilion that caught the imagination of the fair organizers. Again, Weisgal succeeded in attracting record-breaking crowds, this time to what he claimed was "the first Palestine exhibit at an international exposition in the United States."[81] The presence of Albert Einstein at the opening helped produce the largest single day's attendance in the history of the fair, according to Weisgal, who estimated that more than two million people visited the pavilion in all.[82] The crowds were in no small measure a result of the massive, and relentless, public relations, fundraising, and publicity campaign that Weisgal mounted through the American Jewish community. The Pavilion was a vehicle for mobilizing American Jewry in support of the larger Zionist cause.

Weisgal characterized the Palestine Pavilion as "showmanship of another kind."[83] The major bone of contention was its location on the Flushing Meadows fairgrounds:

One section had been set aside for the

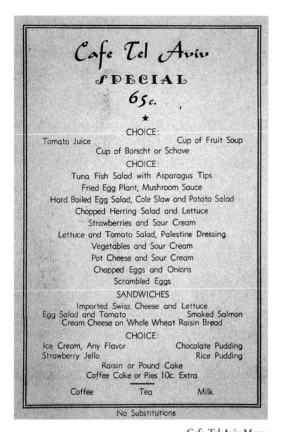

Cafe Tel Aviv

SPECIAL

65c.

★

CHOICE:
Tomato Juice   Cup of Fruit Soup
Cup of Borscht or Schave

CHOICE:
Tuna Fish Salad with Asparagus Tips
Fried Egg Plant, Mushroom Sauce
Hard Boiled Egg Salad, Cole Slaw and Potato Salad
Chopped Herring Salad and Lettuce
Strawberries and Sour Cream
Lettuce and Tomato Salad, Palestine Dressing
Vegetables and Sour Cream
Pot Cheese and Sour Cream
Chopped Eggs and Onions
Scrambled Eggs

SANDWICHES
Imported Swiss Cheese and Lettuce
Egg Salad and Tomato   Smoked Salmon
Cream Cheese on Whole Wheat Raisin Bread

CHOICE:
Ice Cream, Any Flavor   Chocolate Pudding
Strawberry Jello   Rice Pudding
Raisin or Pound Cake
Coffee Cake or Pies 10c. Extra

Coffee   Tea   Milk

No Substitutions

Cafe Tel Aviv Menu
New York World's Fair, 1939
With the exception, perhaps, of "Palestine dressing" on their salads, visitors to this eatery on the fairgrounds consumed the familiar cuisine of an American Jewish dairy restaurant, rather than more exotic Middle Eastern fare.

Collection of Peter H. Schweitzer

national pavilions, and that is where I wanted us to be. There was of course no Jewish State as yet, but I believed in its impending arrival on the scene of history, and I wanted the idea of Jewish sovereignty to be anticipated there, in Flushing Meadows.[84]

The design of the Jewish Palestine Pavilion and its contents was in accord with Weisgal's desires, which was "something authentically Palestinian" to show

that "in 1938 Jewish Palestine was a reality; its towns, villages, schools, hospitals and cultural institutions had risen in a land that until our coming had been derelict and waste."[85] Only after objections that the Palestine Pavilion did not represent Arabs in Palestine did Weisgal agree to change its name to Jewish Palestine Pavilion. Insisting—with no trace of irony—that the pavilion should steer clear of politics, Weisgal applied himself to the "construction of the Jewish State under the shadow of the Trylon and Perisphere, or, as the Jews were fond of calling it, the Lulav and Esrog."[86] Winning the battle over location at the fair was critical to the success of Weisgal's construction: "Located as we were on the borderline of the National Pavilions, there was always some question as to whether or not we really 'belonged.'"[87] The exhibits in the Jewish Palestine Pavilion, by following the model of national buildings, simulated the state before it was legally formed. Indeed, as Weisgal pointed out, "In one particular respect, the Palestine Pavilion is unique: It is a national exhibit not sponsored by a government."[88]

In striking contrast with the earlier exhibitions of Biblical antiquities and religion organized by Cyrus Adler, there was no room in the Jewish Palestine Pavilion for ceremonial art created in the diaspora. During the late 1930s, Benjamin and Rose Mintz, "ardent Zionists and devout Jews," attempted to leave Poland. They had applied for a visa to visit America and had been refused. Benjamin was an antique dealer and collector who had amassed a fine collection of Judaica. Max M. Korshak had the idea that, if the collection could be exhibited at the New York World's Fair, the Mintzes might get temporary visas to accompany the objects. Their intention was to settle permanently in Palestine, using money gained from the sale of the collection in America. They were unable to realize their plan, however, because the market was depressed at the time. Korshak proposed the inclusion of the Mintz collection in the Palestine Pavilion, which Weisgal rejected. According to

Korshak, "Mr. Weisgal felt, for some reason that I never understood, that the collection was not suitable as a Palestinian Exhibit since the articles were not products of Palestine, although he did admit that it was a product of the Jewish heritage."[89] The collection and the Mintzes were allowed out of Poland in anticipation of the exhibit, but the objects were never shown at the fair. They were stored in a warehouse and later purchased for the Jewish Museum.

The Jewish Palestine Pavilion was in keeping with the World of the Future theme of the New York World's Fair, a factor in its acceptance by fair organizers. At the same time, fixtures of earlier fairs were either eliminated or reconceived—Weisgal also proposed a pageant, which was not accepted.[90] Located right next to the Jewish Palestine Pavilion, the Temple of Religion was to embody the general theme of religion, rather than feature ongoing exhibitions of particular denominations. In this way, New York's Temple of Religion distinguished itself from the Hall of Religions at the 1933 Century of Progress fair in Chicago and the Temple of Religion at the Golden Gate International Exposition in San Francisco in 1939, both of which featured exhibits of specific religions.[91]

The Women's League of the United Synagogue of America, representing Conservative Judaism, presented a pageant at the 1939 New York World's Fair, entitled *The Jewish Home Beautiful.* The Women's League explicitly distinguished their presentation from a "museum piece," which is just "something to admire and then to forget, or merely to recall in conversation."[92] For them, as for Weisgal,

the fair offered a platform for advocacy: they urged Jewish women to "create new glory and new beauty for the Jewish home," thereby transforming the "humblest surroundings into a sanctuary more holy and beautiful than the house decorated elaborately, but without love and intelligence and religious warmth."[93] The world of tomorrow would include not only a Jewish homeland in Palestine, but also a Jewish home right in the heart of suburban America. Its table would be set with a Jewish National Fund box, Jaffa oranges, and other evidence of support for a Jewish homeland elsewhere.

Whether they provided models of an ancient past or models for a future Jewish state or American Jewish home, Jews first had to negotiate the space of display. The geography of the fair, on the ground and in the imagination of fairgoers, was highly charged. One space was several places, nowhere more vividly than in such designations as Holy Land, Bible lands, Eretz Israel, Zion, Filastin, Palestine, and the State of Israel. In the spaces of display and their uneasy alignment with the geopiety and geopolitics of the region designated as the Holy Land, Jews were a Bible people, witnesses to the world of Jesus, performers of the sultan's delights, and prototype of the Semitic race. They were also modern Americans professing a universalistic religion and ardent Zionists committed to the creation of a Jewish homeland in Palestine. By the eve of World War II, they had learned how to use the medium of a world's fair to make a place for themselves in the world.

Notes

I would like to thank Grace Cohen Grossman for so generously sharing her expertise, Peter Cherches for his expert research assistance, Andrew Davis for the gift of *Portrait Types of the Midway Plaisance,* and Zachary Baker for pointing out useful sources. Research for this essay was conducted while I was a Winston Fellow at the Institute for Advanced Studies at the Hebrew University in Jerusalem in 1996 and part of a research group, Visual Culture and Modern Jewish Society, convened by Richard Cohen and Ezra Mendelsohn.

[1] Emil G. Hirsch, "Elements of Universal Religion," in John Henry Barrows, ed., *The World's Parliament of Religions: An Illustrated History of the World's First Parliament of Religions, Held in Chicago in Connection With the Columbian Exposition of 1893* (Chicago: Parliament Publishing Company, 1893), p. 1304.

[2] Joseph Silverman, "Popular Errors About the Jews," in *World's Parliament of Religions,* p. 1121.

[3] F. Opper, "Human Natur'," *World's Fair Puck* 18 (4 December 1893), pp. 210-11.

[4] On the notion of flexible positional superiority as a strategy of Orientalism, see Edward Said, *Orientalism* (New York: Random House, 1978), p. 7.

[5] See *The Book of the Exile,* Souvenir of the Bazaar and Fair held under the auspices of the People's Relief Committee for the Jewish War Sufferers (New York City, 1916), p. 21.

[6] On the difference between "models of" and "models for," see Clifford Geertz, "Religion As a Cultural System," *The Interpretation of Cultures* (New York: Basic Books, 1973), p. 93 ff.

[7] Silverman, "Popular Errors About the Jews," p. 1121.

[8] Hirsch, "Elements of Universal Religion," p. 1304.

[9] "The City," *The American Hebrew,* 16 June 1893.

[10] Editorial, *The Reform Advocate,* 22 July 1893, pp. 441-42.

[11] John Henry Barrows, "The Assembling of the Parliament—Words of Welcome and Fellowship," in *World's Parliament of Religions,* p. 72.

[12] Barrows, "Grandeur and Final Influence of the Parliament," *World's Parliament of Religions,* p. 1573.

[13] Barrows, "Assembling of the Parliament," p. 74.

[14] D.G. Lyon, "Jewish Contributions to Civilization," in *World's Parliament of Religions,* p. 817.

[15] Silverman, "Popular Errors About the Jews," p. 1120.

[16] See Maurice Olender, *The Languages of Paradise: Race, Religion, and Philology in the Nineteenth Century,* trans. Arthur Goldhammer (Cambridge: Harvard University Press, 1992).

[17] "Speech of P.C. Mozoomdar," in *World's Parliament of Religions,* p. 87.

[18] Lyon, "Jewish Contributions to Civilization," pp. 826, 828.

[19] Silverman, "Popular Errors About the Jews," p. 1121.

[20] Lyon, "Jewish Contributions to Civilization," p. 819.

[21] Cyrus Adler, "Museum Collections to Illustrate Religious History and Ceremony," in U.S. Congress, House of Representatives, *Miscellaneous Documents, 53rd Cong., 2d sess., 1893-1894,* vol. 30 (Washington, D.C.: Government Printing Office, 1895), pp. 755-68; Morris Jastrow, "Recent Movements in the Historical Study of Religions in America," *The Biblical World,* new series 1 (January-June 1893): 24-32.

[22] Isidor Lewi, "Yom Kippur on the Midway," *Report of the Committee on Awards of the World's Columbian Commission,* Special Reports Upon Special Subjects or Groups, vol. 2 (Washington, D.C., Government Printing Office, 1901), p. 1693.

[23] The definitive study of the history of Judaica at the Smithsonian Institution and Adler's role in forming the collection is Grace Cohen Grossman with Richard Eighme Ahlborn, *Judaica at the Smithsonian: Cultural Politics As Cultural Model,* Smithsonian Studies in History and Technology, no. 52 (Washington, D.C.: Smithsonian Institution Press, 1997).

[24] Department of Publicity and Promotion, ed., *World's Columbian Exposition, 1893, Official Catalogue, United States Government Building,* part XVI (Chicago: W.B. Conkey Company, Publishers to the World's Columbian Exposition, 1893), pp. 141-42.

[25] Cyrus Adler and I. M. Casanowicz, *The Collection of Jewish Ceremonial Objects in the United States National Museum.* From the Proceedings of the United States National Museum, vol. 35 (Washington, D.C.: Government Printing Office, 1908), p. 701.

[26] *Di velt oysshtelung in Tshikago in 1893,* in the Hebrew Union College Library, Cincinnati, pp. 5-6. I would like to thank Beth Wenger for bringing this rare publication to my attention.

[27] *Ibid,* p. 5.

[28] The article appeared 6 September 1894 and was reprinted as Appendix IV, in Adler, "Museum Collections to Illustrate Religious History and Ceremonies," pp. 766-67.

[29] Grossman, *Judaica at the Smithsonian,* p. 52.

[30] See Grossman, *Judaica at the Smithsonian* for a detailed account of the history and names of each section.

[31] Cyrus Adler, "Report on the Section of Oriental Antiquities in the U.S. National Museum, 1889," *United States National Museum Report for 1888-1889* (Washington, D.C.: Government Printing Office, 1890), p. 289.

[32] Cyrus Adler, "Report on the Section of Oriental Antiquities in the U.S. National Museum, 1888," *United States*

National Museum Annual Report for 1888 (Washington, D.C.: Government Printing Office, 1890), p. 94.

33 *Ibid.*

34 *Ibid.*, pp. 94-95.

35 Cyrus Adler and I.M. Casanowicz, *Biblical Antiquities: A Description of the Exhibit at the Cotton States International Exposition, Atlanta, 1895.* From the Report of the United States National Museum for 1896 (Washington, D.C.: Smithsonian Institution, 1898), pp. 989-99.

36 *Ibid.*, p. 948.

37 Letter from Cyrus Adler to Professor S.P. Langley, Secretary of the Smithsonian Institution, 16 February 1888, Smithsonian Institution Archives, Record Unit 201, Box 11.

38 Adler, *Biblical Antiquities*, pp. 945-49; "Exhibit at the Cotton States Exposition, Department of Oriental Antiquities and Religious Ceremonial," *Smithsonian Institution Annual Report for 1895-1896* (Washington, D.C.: Government Printing Office, [1898]), p. 629.

39 R. Edward Earll, "Appendix A: Report upon the Exhibit of the Smithsonian Institution, Including the U.S. National Museum, at the Centennial Exposition of the Ohio Valley and Central States, Held at Cincinnati, Ohio, in 1888," in G.B. Goode, Report of the Assistant Secretary, *Annual Report of the Board of Regents of the Smithsonian Institution, 1889,* Appendix A (Washington, D.C.: Government Printing Office, 1891), p. 165.

40 Cyrus Adler, "The Living Past," *Lectures, Selected Papers, Addresses* (Philadelphia: Privately printed, 1933), p. 159.

41 Lewi, "Yom Kippur on the Midway," p. 1693.

42 See Sol Bloom, *The Autobiography of Sol Bloom* (New York: G.P. Putnam's Sons, 1948).

43 *Oriental and Occidental Northern and Southern Portrait Types of the Midway Plaisance* (St. Louis: N.D. Thompson, 1894), with an introduction by F.W. Putnam.

44 Cyrus Adler, *I Remember the Days* (Philadelphia: Jewish Publication Society of America, 1941), p. 75.

45 *Ibid.*, pp. 132-33.

46 Denton J. Snider, *World's Fair Studies* (Chicago: Sigma Publishing Co., 1895), p. 373.

47 "Object to Bloomers," *Chicago Daily Tribune,* 5 May 1893, p. 1.

48 *Ibid.* See also Jeanne Madeline Weimann, *The Fair Women* (Chicago: Academy Chicago, 1981), p. 532 ff.

49 *Oriental and Occidental Northern and Southern Portrait Types,* title page.

50 See Julie K. Brown, *Contesting Images: Photography and the World's Columbian Exposition* (Tucson: University of Arizona Press, 1994), p. 78 ff.

51 *Ibid.*, p. 82 ff.

52 *Ibid.*, pp. 45-46. See also Robert W. Rydell, *All the World's a Fair: Visions of Empire at American International Expositions, 1876-1916* (Chicago: University of Chicago Press, 1984), p. 57.

53 Alan Sekula, "The Body and the Archive," *October* 39 (1986): 3-64.

54 *Oriental and Occidental Northern and Southern Portrait Types,* n.p.

55 *Ibid.*

56 Adler, *I Remember the Days,* p. 136.

57 *Oriental and Occidental Northern and Southern Portrait Types,* n.p.

58 See John J. Wayne, "Constantinople to Chicago: In the Footsteps of Far-Away Moses," *Library of Congress Information Bulletin* 51: 1 (13 January 1992): 14-21.

59 *Ibid.*

60 Jerusalem Exhibit Co., *World's Fair Souvenir Album of Jerusalem* (St. Louis: Towers & Co., [1903]).

61 John Heyl Vincent and James W. Lee, *Earthly Footsteps of the Man of Galilee: Being Four Hundred Original Photographic Views and Descriptions of the Places Connected with the Early Life of Our Lord and his Apostles, Traced with Note Book and Camera, Showing where Christ was born, brought up, baptized, tempted, transfigured and crucified, Together with the scenes of his prayers, tears, miracles and sermons, and also places made sacred by the labors of his Apostles, from Jerusalem to Rome* (St. Louis: N.D. Thompson, 1895). See John Davis, *The Landscape of Belief: Encountering the Holy Land in Nineteenth-Century American Art and Culture* (Princeton: Princeton University Press, 1996); Lester I. Vogel, *To See a Promised Land: Americans and the Holy Land in the Nineteenth Century* (University Park: Pennsylvania State University Press, 1993); and Yeshayahu Nir, *The Bible and the Image: The History of Photography in the Holy Land 1839-1899* (Philadelphia: University of Pennsylvania Press, 1985).

62 F.E. Peters, "The Procession That Never Was: The Painful Way of Jerusalem," *The Drama Review,* Special Issue on

Processional Performance, eds. Brooks McNamara and Barbara Kirshenblatt-Gimblett, 29: 3 (T107) (1985): 31-41.

63 Vogel, *To See a Promised Land,* p. 11.

64 Jerusalem Exhibit Company, *Prospectus of The Jerusalem Exhibit Co. Organized for the purpose of reproducing at the St. Louis World's Fair (Louisiana Purchase Exhibition) In 1904, a reproduction of the most interesting features of the City of Jerusalem* (St. Louis: The Jerusalem Exhibit Co., [1902]), p. 11.

65 *Ibid.,* p. 9.

66 James W. Lee, "Jerusalem at the World's Fair," in *Prospectus of The Jerusalem Exhibit Co.,* p. 18.

67 *Prospectus of The Jerusalem Exhibit Co.,* p. 10.

68 See Davis, *Landscape of Belief,* p. 92 ff.

69 Letter from Rev. Samuel I. Lindsay, Secretary of the Jerusalem Exhibit Company, to Rev. L. Grossman in Cincinnati, 27 January 1903. This and other such appeals to Grossman are attached to the prospectus in the Hebrew Union College Library, Cincinnati.

70 Montefiore Bienenstok, "The Jews of the World's Fair City," *The New Era* 4:6 (May 1904), p. 343. I would like to thank Susan Miller for bringing this source to my attention.

71 *Ibid.,* pp. 338, 349.

72 *Ibid.,* p. 343.

73 *Prospectus of The Jerusalem Exhibit Co.,* p. 9.

74 Herman Melville, *Journal of a Visit to Europe and the Levant, October 11, 1856-May 6, 1857,* edited by Howard C. Horsford (Princeton: Princeton University Press, 1955), p. 154.

75 Nathaniel Burt, quoted by Vogel, *To See a Promised Land,* p. 83.

76 *Prospectus of The Jerusalem Exhibit Co.,* p. 11.

77 *Ibid.*

78 *Ibid.,* p. 17.

79 See Atay Citron, "Pageantry and Theater in the Service of Jewish Nationalism, 1933-1946," Ph.D. diss., New York University, 1990.

80 Meyer W. Weisgal, *Meyer Weisgal . . . So Far: An Autobiography* (New York: Random House, 1971), p. 147.

81 Meyer Weisgal, ed., *Palestine Book* (official publication of the Jewish Palestine Pavilion at the New York World's Fair 1939) (New York: Pavilion Publications, Inc., 1939), p. 41. I would like to thank Robert Rothstein for making his copy of this book available to me.

82 Weisgal, *...So Far,* p. 148.

83 *Ibid.,* p. 142.

84 *Ibid.,* p. 149.

85 *Ibid.,* p. 150.

86 *Ibid.,* pp. 158, 161.

87 *Ibid.,* p. 161.

88 Weisgal, *Palestine Book,* p. 41.

89 Letter from Max M. Korshak to Dr. Stephen Kayser, 21 February 1950, Mintz File, The Jewish Museum, New York.

90 Equally interesting are the proposals that were rejected. See Susan Miller, "The Selling of Zion: Eretz Israel at the 1939 New York World's Fair" (Unpublished paper, 1994).

91 See Jesse T. Todd, "Goodwill in the World of Tomorrow: Imagining the Future of American Religion at the New York World's Fair, 1939-1940," Ph.D. diss., Columbia University, 1996.

92 Betty D. Greenberg and Althea O. Silverman, *The Jewish Home Beautiful* (New York: National Women's League of the United States Synagogue of America, [1941] 1953), pp. 13-14. A second pageant, *The Lamp of Liberty,* was performed in the Temple of Religion on 31 July 1940 and sponsored by the New York Metropolitan Section of the Jewish Welfare Board.

93 *Ibid.*

Checklist of the Exhibition

Prologue

"Map of the world in the shape of a cloverleaf"
from *Itinerarium Sacrae Scripturae*
by Heinrich Bünting, 1581
photoreproduction from Dan Behat and Shalom Sabar,
Jerusalem, Stone and Spirit: 3000 Years of History and Art
[Tel Aviv]: Matan Arts Publishers Ltd., 1997
Center for Judaic Studies,
University of Pennsylvania Library

"The Way to the Holy Lande"
Information for Pilgrims unto the Holy Land, 1524
photoreproduction from a facsimile edition edited by
Gordon E. Duff
London: Lawrence & Bullen, 1893
University of Pennsylvania Library

Map of the City of Jerusalem
Theatrum Terrae Sanctae et Biblicarum Historiarum
by Christiaan Van Adrichem
Köln, 1600
Center for Judaic Studies,
University of Pennsylvania Library

Map of the Exodus from Egypt to Canaan
by Abraham bar Ja'akob
Haggadah shel Pesah, Amsterdam, 1695
Dr. Ierach and Dalia Daskal

Historical Map of Palestine or the Holy Land
drawn by J.T. Assheton
Philadelphia: S. Augustus Mitchell, [ca. 1835?]
Center for Judaic Studies,
University of Pennsylvania Library

Mizrah
lithograph, ca. 1900
National Museum of American Jewish History
Gift of Mr. and Mrs. Paul Schimmel

View of Jerusalem
by Frans Hogenberg, Köln, 1588
Dr. Ierach and Dalia Daskal

Engraving of the American consulate in Jerusalem
1872
photoreproduction from *Ariel: A Quarterly Review,* 1969
University of Pennsylvania Library

Map of US towns with Biblical names
based on Moshe Davis, *America and the Holy Land: With
Eyes Toward Zion-IV*
(Westport, Conn,: Praeger Publishers, 1995)

**Description of a View of the City of Jerusalem
and the Surrounding Country**
by F. Catherwood
New York: William Osborn, 1845
Center for Judaic Studies,
University of Pennsylvania Library

Stone from the Third Wall of Jerusalem
discovered ca. 1926
Center for Judaic Studies,
University of Pennsylvania Library

Scale drawing of the Third Wall of Jerusalem
by E.L. Sukenik and L. A. Mayer, *The Third Wall of
Jerusalem: An Account of Excavations*
London: Oxford University Press, 1930
photoreproduction
Center for Judaic Studies,
University of Pennsylvania Library

Visiting the Holy Land

Cook's Tourists' Handbook for Palestine and Syria
by Thomas Cook
London: Thomas Cook & Son, 1876
University of Pennsylvania Library

Ancient Jerusalem: Pictorial Palestine
by M. Avi-Yonah
pamphlet, Jerusalem: Emil Pikovsky for Zionist
Organizations Youth Department, 1930
Center for Judaic Studies,
University of Pennsylvania Library

Advertisement for Cook's Tour
The New Palestine, 27 March 1925
photoreproduction
Center for Judaic Studies,
University of Pennsylvania Library

Advertisement for Mauretania, Cunard Line
The New Palestine, 4-11 January 1929
photoreproduction
Center for Judaic Studies,
University of Pennsylvania Library

Advertisement for Holland American Line
The American Hebrew, 22 November 1929
photoreproduction
Center for Judaic Studies,
University of Pennsylvania Library

"President Arthur Zion's Ship"
by Solomon Small
New York: A. Teres, 1925
National Museum of American Jewish History
Gift of Robert and Molly Freedman

Travel brochure
Times Square Travel Bureau, New York, 1932-1933
American Jewish Historical Society,
Waltham, Mass., and New York, N.Y.

Travel brochure
Travel Institute for Bible Research, March 1930
Visual Collections, Fine Arts Library, Harvard University

"Erez-Israel Palestine" Map
Rosen tours, New York, n.d.
Center for Judaic Studies,
University of Pennsylvania Library

Photograph of Farewell to Rabbi Schussheim
Providence, Rhode Island, 1929
Farley, photographer
photoreproduction
Joseph and Miriam Ratner Center for the Study of
Conservative Judaism
Jewish Theological Seminary of America

Tourist map of Jaffa and Tel Aviv, Haifa and Jerusalem
MobiLubrication Stations
Peter H. Schweitzer

A Guide to Jewish Palestine
second edition
Jerusalem: Keren Kayemeth LeIsrael and Keren Hayesod,
1927
Peter H. Schweitzer

Advertisement for Palestine Railway
Guide to New Palestine, ninth edition
Jerusalem: Benjamin Lewensohn for the Zionist
Information Bureau for Tourists in Palestine, 1936-1937
photoreproduction
Center for Judaic Studies,
University of Pennsylvania Library

Advertisement for King David Hotel
Guide to New Palestine, ninth edition
Jerusalem: Benjamin Lewensohn for the Zionist
Information Bureau for Tourists in Palestine, 1936-1937
photoreproduction
Center for Judaic Studies,
University of Pennsylvania Library

Madrikh Eretz-Yisrael
by Zev Vilnay
Tel Aviv: HaPoel Hatzair, 1941
Center for Judaic Studies,
University of Pennsylvania Library

"Notice for Tourists about Safety of Water"
Pamphlet
Jerusalem, 1924
Visual Collections, Fine Arts Library, Harvard University

Luggage Tag
Nairn Transport. Co.
Palestine, n.d.
Visual Collections, Fine Arts Library, Harvard University

Brief Guide to Al-Haram Al-Sharif Jerusalem
Jerusalem: Supreme Moslem Council, 1925
Center for Judaic Studies,
University of Pennsylvania Library

Photograph of Jaffa Gate
Jerusalem, late nineteenth century
photoreproduction
Bonfils Studio
University of Pennsylvania Museum

Photograph of tourists and guide on horseback
Palestine(?), ca. 1900
photoreproduction
Visual Collections, Fine Arts Library, Harvard University

Photograph of tourists in palanquins
Palestine, 1890
photoreproduction
Visual Collections, Fine Arts Library, Harvard University

Photograph of airplane in Palestine airport
Palestine, ca. 1930
photoreproduction
YIVO Institute for Jewish Research

Itinerary of trip to Palestine
Abe and Helen Ferst
Jerusalem, 1925
Stanley D. and Elaine L. Ferst

Letter from Abe and Helen Ferst on stationery from Hotel J. Amdursky
Jerusalem, 1925
Stanley D. and Elaine L. Ferst

Photograph of Abe and Helen Ferst in carriage
Egypt, 1925
photoreproduction
Stanley D. and Elaine L. Ferst

Postcard from Hotel Balfouria
Tel Aviv, 1925
Stanley D. and Elaine L. Ferst

Photographs of David Bloom's trip to Palestine
Palestine, 1923
YIVO Institute for Jewish Research

Advertisement for Hanania Bro. Camera Shop
Guide to New Palestine, ninth edition
Jerusalem: Benjamin Lewensohn for the Zionist
Information Bureau for Tourists in Palestine, 1936-1937
photoreproduction
Center for Judaic Studies,
University of Pennsylvania Library

Film footage of Beecher family trip to Palestine
ca. 1920s
videoreproduction
YIVO Institute for Jewish Research

Postcards of scenes of Palestine
Peter H. Schweitzer

Postcards of scenes of Palestine
Baden, Germany, ca. 1900
Paul Hommel, photographer
Center for Judaic Studies,
University of Pennsylvania Library

Postcard with map of Palestine
early 20th century
National Museum of American Jewish History

Brochure for Vester and Co., the American Colony Stores
Jerusalem, ca. 1920s
Visual Collections, Fine Arts Library, Harvard University

Photograph of souvenir booth
Jerusalem, n.d.
photoreproduction
YIVO Institute for Jewish Research

Advertisement for olivewood souvenirs
Hebrew-Christian Quarterly, January 1904
Peter H. Schweitzer

Olivewood Scroll of Esther
Palestine, n.d.
Isaac Pollak

Olivewood spicebox
Palestine, n.d.
Rela Mintz Geffen.

Book of flowers from the Holy Land (untitled)
Jerusalem: Atallah Georges Fréres, ca. 1900
Center for Judaic Studies,
University of Pennsylvania Library

"Wild Flowers of the Holy Land"
Jerusalem, ca. 1900
Center for Judaic Studies,
University of Pennsylvania Library

Gavel made of four types of wood
Palestine, n.d.
Peter H. Schweitzer

Bible with silver cover, Bezalel School of Arts
and Crafts
Jerusalem, 1919
Peter H. Schweitzer

Memorial lamp in the shape of Tomb of Rachel
Palestine, n.d.
Isaac Pollak

Bag of soil from Mount of Olives
General Burial Society
Jerusalem, n.d.
National Museum of American Jewish History

Seashell with engraving, "Sheyndl Sarah"
Palestine, n.d.
Peter H. Schweitzer

Oil lamp
Palestine, ca. 1900
Semitic Museum, Harvard University

Pitcher made of brass and pewter
Palestine, ca. 1900
Semitic Museum, Harvard University

Pair of hand-shaped amulets
Palestine, ca. 1900
Semitic Museum, Harvard University

Bead necklace made of blue glass
Palestine, ca. 1900
Semitic Museum, Harvard University

Stone cup
Palestine, ca. 1900
Semitic Museum, Harvard University

Stone bowl
Palestine, ca. 1900
Semitic Museum, Harvard University

Plaster model of Tomb of Rachel
Palestine, ca. 1900
Semitic Museum, Harvard University

Plaster model of Tomb of Absalom
Palestine, ca. 1900
Semitic Museum, Harvard University

Ceramic tile with Arabic calligraphy
Palestine, ca. 1900
Semitic Museum, Harvard University

Sidonian shells
Palestine, ca. 1900
Semitic Museum, Harvard University

The Innocents Abroad; or, The New Pilgrims' Progress
first edition, by Samuel Clemens (Mark Twain)
Hartford, Conn.: American Publishing. Co., 1869
University of Pennsylvania Library

Photograph of Louis Brandeis
Palestine, 1919
photoreproduction
Central Zionist Archives, Jerusalem

Photograph of Henrietta Szold and staff of AZMU at
tree planting ceremony
Palestine, ca. 1920
photoreproduction
Hadassah, The Women's Zionist Organization
of America

"Scenes from Tel Aviv,"
Jewish Daily Forward 29 November 1925
Palestine, 1925
Alter Kacyzne, photographer
photoreproduction
YIVO Institute for Jewish Research

"Pictures of Jewish Life and Characters,"
Jewish Daily Forward 6 December 1925
Palestine, 1925
Alter Kacyzne, photographer
photoreproduction
YIVO Institute for Jewish Research

Palestine: a bazukh in yor 1925 un in 1929
by Abraham Cahan
New York: Forward Association, 1934
Center for Judaic Studies,
University of Pennsylvania Library

Photograph of John Fitzgerald Kennedy
Palestine, 1939
Zvi Oron, photographer
photoreproduction
Central Zionist Archives, Jerusalem

Underwood Travel System
New York: Underwood & Underwood, 1913
Visual Collections, Fine Arts Library, Harvard University

Traveling in the Holy Land Through the Stereoscope by
Jesse Lyman Hurlbut
New York: Underwood & Underwood, 1900
Visual Collections, Fine Arts Library, Harvard University

Stereopticon, "Measuring Wheat in the Biblical Way"
Philadelphia: Universal Photo Art Co., ca. 1900
YIVO Institute for Jewish Research

Stereopticon, "Looking East from Joppa Gate"
Philadelphia: C.H. Graves, 1903
YIVO Institute for Jewish Research

Stereopticon, "The Church of the Holy Sepulcher"
ca. 1900
YIVO Institute for Jewish Research

Stereopticon, "A Jerusalem Jew"
London: Frank M. Good, ca. 1900
YIVO Institute for Jewish Research

Stereopticon of men working in fields
ca. 1900
YIVO Institute for Jewish Research

Stereopticon, "Market Place in Jaffa"
Palestine, n.d.
Peter H. Schweitzer

Stereopticon, "Jerusalem Jews at the Wailing Place"
New York: Underwood & Underwood, 1896
Peter H. Schweitzer

Reproduction of lantern slide, "Mount of Olives From
City Wall"
American Colony Photographers, Vester & Co.
Jerusalem, ca. 1900
Center for Judaic Studies,
University of Pennsylvania Library

Reproduction of lantern slide, "Looking Up the
River Jordan"
American Colony Photographers, Vester & Co.
Jerusalem, ca. 1900
Center for Judaic Studies,
University of Pennsylvania Library

Reproduction of lantern slide, "Christian Street"
American Colony Photographers, Vester & Co.
Jerusalem, ca. 1900
Center for Judaic Studies,
University of Pennsylvania Library

Reproduction of lantern slide, "View of Bethlehem
from the West"
American Colony Photographers, Vester & Co.
Jerusalem, ca. 1900
Center for Judaic Studies,
University of Pennsylvania Library

Reproduction of lantern slide, "Absalom's Pillar"
American Colony Photographers, Vester & Co.
Jerusalem, ca. 1900
Center for Judaic Studies,
University of Pennsylvania Library

Photograph of "Jews' Wailing Place"
Jerusalem, late nineteenth century
Bonfils Studio
photoreproduction
University of Pennsylvania Museum

*Tramping Through Palestine: Impressions of an
American Student in Israeland*
by Milton Goell
New York: Kensington Press, 1926
Center for Judaic Studies,
University of Pennsylvania Library

Fun Nyu-York biz Rekhovos un tsurik
by Yehoash (Solomon Bloomgarten)
New York : Hebrew Publishing Co., 1917
Center for Judaic Studies,
University of Pennsylvania Library

The Feet of the Messenger
by Yehoash (Solomon Bloomgarten)
Philadelphia: Jewish Publication Society of America,
1923
Center for Judaic Studies,
University of Pennsylvania Library

Palestine: The Holy Land as It Was and as It Is,
by John Fulton
Philadelphia: Henry T. Coates & Co., 1900
Center for Judaic Studies,
University of Pennsylvania Library

The Modern Magic Carpet: Air-Jaunting Over the Ancient Near East
by Marie Beale
Baltimore: J. H. Furst, 1930
Center for Judaic Studies,
University of Pennsylvania Library

A Ride on Horseback Through the Holy Land Written for the Children
by L.L.A.
Boston: Henry Hoyt, 1874
University of Pennsylvania Library

Representing the Holy Land

Print of the Temple of Solomon
"Taken from the model erected by Councillor Schott at Hamburg"
Philadelphia: Jacob N. Taylor & Co., 1868
National Museum of American Jewish History
Gift of Meyer H. and Sophie M. Sklar

Photographs of model of the Temple Mount
from Conrad Schick, *Beit el Makdas, oder Der alte Tempelplatz zu Jerusalem,* Jerusalem, 1887
photoreproductions
Center for Judaic Studies,
University of Pennsylvania Library

Section of Conrad Schick's model of the Temple Mount
Jerusalem (?), ca. 1885
Semitic Museum, Harvard University

Photograph of "Palestine Park"
Chautauqua, N.Y., ca. 1880
photoreproduction
Chautauqua Assembly

Map of "Palestine Park"
from *Guide Book to Palestine Park*
Chautauqua, N.Y.: Chautauqua Press, 1936
photoreproduction
Chautauqua Assembly

Model of Old City of Jerusalem
by Moses Kernoosh (?)
Ann Arbor, Mich., ca. 1880
American Jewish Historical Society,
Waltham, Mass., and New York, N.Y.

Model of Jerusalem and environs
Vester and Co., The American Colony
Jerusalem, ca. 1900
Semitic Museum, Harvard University

Architectural designs for model of Temple of Solomon
by John Wesley Kelchner, Helme and Corbett Architects
New York, 1913
photoreproductions
Center for Judaic Studies,
University of Pennsylvania Library

Photograph of Jacob Jehuda with his model of the Temple of Solomon
Jewish Palestine Pavilion, New York World's Fair, 1939
photoreproduction
Archives, Weizmann Institute of Science, Rehovot

Invitation to opening of Semitic Museum, Harvard University
Cambridge, Mass., 1903
Semitic Museum, Harvard University

"Catalog of Exhibits," Semitic Museum, Harvard University
Cambridge, Mass., 1903
Semitic Museum, Harvard University

Photograph of Palestinian Room, Semitic Museum, Harvard University
Cambridge, Mass., 1903
photoreproduction
Semitic Museum, Harvard University

Photograph of costume display, Semitic Museum, Harvard University
Cambridge, Mass., 1903
photoreproduction
Semitic Museum, Harvard University

Embroidered jacket
Bethlehem, ca. 1900
Semitic Museum, Harvard University

Children's shoes
Palestine, ca. 1900
Semitic Museum, Harvard University

Man's robe
Northern Palestine, ca. 1900
Semitic Museum, Harvard University

Embroidered hat
Palestine, ca. 1900
Semitic Museum, Harvard University

Headdress
Palestine, ca. 1900
Semitic Museum, Harvard University

Map of Palestine showing location of Beth-Shan
Museum Journal (Philadelphia), March 1929
photoreproduction
University of Pennsylvania Museum

Map of Excavations at Beth-Shan
Palestine, ca. 1921-1923
Clarence Fisher (?)
University of Pennsylvania Museum

Watercolor of mosaic from Beth-Shan
Palestine, 1923
Ahmed Yousef (?)
University of Pennsylvania Museum

Photograph of excavation at Beth-Shan
Palestine, 1925
photoreproduction
University of Pennsylvania Museum

Glass flask
Roman Period, found at Beth-Shan
University of Pennsylvania Museum

String of glass beads
Roman Period, found at Beth-Shan
University of Pennsylvania Museum

Basalt bowl
Iron Age, found at Beth-Shan
University of Pennsylvania Museum

Pottery bowl
Iron Age II, found at Beth-Shan
University of Pennsylvania Museum

Oil lamp
Sixth Century CE, found at Beth-Shan
University of Pennsylvania Museum

Photograph of Palestinian installation
Philadelphia, 1926
photoreproduction
University of Pennsylvania Museum

Brochure, "Down the Steps of History at Biblical Beth-Shan"
Philadelphia, ca. 1933
University of Pennsylvania Museum

Biblical Antiquities: A Description of the Exhibit at the Cotton States International Exposition, Atlanta, 1895
by Cyrus Adler and I.M. Casanowicz
Washington: Government Printing Office, 1898
Center for Judaic Studies,
University of Pennsylvania Library

Certificate of appointment presented to Special Commissioner Cyrus Adler
1893 World's Colombian Exposition
Chicago, 1891
Center for Judaic Studies,
University of Pennsylvania Library

Photograph of Rahlo Jammele, Jewish Dancing Girl
Portrait Types of the Midway Plaisance, World's Fair Art Series
St. Louis: N.D. Thompson, 12 April 1894
Barbara Kirshenblatt-Gimblett

Cartoon, "Human Natur'"
World's Fair Puck, 4 September 1893
photoreproduction
Yale University Library

Photograph of Jerusalem display
Louisiana Purchase Exposition, St. Louis, Mo., 1904
H.C. White and Co., photographers
photoreproduction
Library of Congress

Booklet, *The Jewish Exhibit*
A Century of Progress, Chicago, 1933-34
National Museum of American Jewish History

Photograph of Palestine display,
A Century of Progress, Chicago, 1934
photoreproduction
Central Zionist Archives, Jerusalem

Fundraising brochure
American Committee for Jewish Palestine
Participation at the New York World's Fair
New York, 1939
Center for Judaic Studies,
University of Pennsylvania Library

Pamphlet, "Palestine Pavilion"
New York World's Fair, 1939
Peter H. Schweitzer

**Typescript of Albert Einstein's speech at
dedication of Jewish Palestine Pavilion**
New York World's Fair, 1939
Peter H. Schweitzer

Postcard of Jewish Palestine Pavilion
New York World's Fair, 1939
National Museum of American Jewish History

Palestine Book
Jewish Palestine Pavilion, New York World's Fair, 1939
National Museum of American Jewish History

Photograph of exterior of Palestine Pavilion
New York, 1939
photoreproduction
Hadassah, The Women's Zionist Organization
of America

Menu, Cafe Tel Aviv
New York, 1939
Peter H. Schweitzer

Sheet music, "A Heim in Palestine,"
by Louis Gilrod and Peretz Sandler
New York: Trio Press, 1925
National Museum of American Jewish History
Gift of Sondra Katz

Sheet music, "I'm Building a Palace in Palestine,"
by Richard Howard
Boston: Daly Music Publisher, 1916
National Museum of American Jewish History

**Advertisement for Kalem Company Motion
Picture Productions**
New York, ca. 1918
photoreproduction
Jacob Rader Marcus Center of the American Jewish
Archives, Cincinnati, Ohio

Photographic still from *Dream of My People*
Palestine, 1934
photoreproduction
Center for Judaic Studies,
University of Pennsylvania Library

Film, "Tourists Embarking at Jaffa"
Thomas Edison, 1903
videoreproduction
Library of Congress

Film, "Jerusalem's Busiest Street"
Thomas Edison, 1903
videoreproduction
Library of Congress

Film excerpt, *Land of Promise*
1935
videoreproduction
National Center for Jewish Film

**Photograph of Samuel Goldenberg as Moses
in** *The Eternal Road* by Franz Werfel and Kurt Weill
New York, 1937
photoreproduction
Weill-Lenya Research Center, Kurt Weill Foundation
for Music, New York

Program for *A Flag is Born*
by Ben Hecht and Kurt Weill
New York, 1946
Weill-Lenya Research Center, Kurt Weill Foundation
for Music, New York

Photograph of *We Will Never Die*
by Ben Hecht and Kurt Weill
New York, 1943
photoreproduction
Weill-Lenya Research Center, Kurt Weill Foundation
for Music, New York

Photograph of *Romance of a People,*
Meyer W. Weisgal, executive director
Chicago, 1933
photoreproduction
Archives, Weizmann Institute of Science, Rehovot

The Pioneers: Scenes from Folk-life in Palestine
by Jacob Weinberg
New York: J. Fischer, 1932
Tuttleman Library of Gratz College

Handbill, "Fifth Bikkurim" dance concert
New York, 1941
92nd Street YM/YWHA Archives

Palestine Dances!
by Corinne Chochem and Muriel Roth
New York: Behrman, 1941
Center for Judaic Studies,
University of Pennsylvania Library

The Bible Story, vol. 2, by Sulamith Ish-Kishor
New York: United Synagogue of America, 1923
Center for Judaic Studies,
University of Pennsylvania Library

The Bible Play Workshop
by Rita Benton
New York and Cincinnati: Abingdon Press, 1923
Center for Judaic Studies,
University of Pennsylvania Library

First Bible Stories
by Jessie Eleanor Moore
New York: Thomas Nelson and Sons, 1929
Center for Judaic Studies,
University of Pennsylvania Library

Photograph of geography classroom
from *A Curriculum for Jewish Religious Schools*
by Rabbi Alter F. Landesman
New York: United Synagogue of America, 1922
photoreproduction
Center for Judaic Studies,
University of Pennsylvania Library

The Haggadah for Children by Rabbi Jacob P. Rudin
New York: Bloch, 1942
Tuttleman Library of Gratz College

Pioneer Songs of Palestine
by Abraham Wolf Binder
New York: Edward B. Marks Music Corporation, 1942
Peter H. Schweitzer

Advertisement for *Songs Heard in Palestine*
by Anna Shomer Rothenberg
Bloch's Book Bulletin, November 1929
photoreproduction
Barbara Kirshenblatt-Gimblett

Arts and Crafts for the Jewish Club
by Harry L. Comins and Ruben Leaf
Cincinnati: Union of American Hebrew
Congregations, 1934
Center for Judaic Studies,
University of Pennsylvania Library

Kindervelt **monthly children's magazine**
Farband/Poale-Zion, June-July 1943
YIVO Institute for Jewish Research Archives

Hebrew school notebook
New York: Hebrew Publishing Company, n.d.
Peter H. Schweitzer

Map of Palestine
"Peerless Series of Sunday School Maps"
St. Louis, Mo.: A.H. Eilers and Company, n.d.
Peter H. Schweitzer

Record album, *Hebrew Songs for Children*
by Seymour Silbermintz and Hannah Harris
New York: Mizrachi National Education
Committee, n.d.
YIVO Institute for Jewish Research Archives

Record album, *Song and Soil/Shirei Ha-moledet*
Sung by United Synagogue Chorus, n.d.
YIVO Institute for Jewish Research Archives

Photograph of girls gardening
Massad Hebrew Camps, ca. 1940s
photoreproduction
Rivka and Shlomo Shulsinger

Hanukkah menorah
Bezalel School of Arts and Crafts
Jerusalem, n.d.
Bella Lewensohn Schafer

Ceramic tile with portrait of Theodor Herzl
Bezalel School of Arts and Crafts
Jerusalem, n.d.
Bella Lewensohn Schafer

Ceramic tile with scene of Western Wall
Bezalel School of Arts and Crafts
Jerusalem, n.d.
Bella Lewensohn Schafer

Haboker **by Saul Raskin**
Painting, oil on canvass
Palestine, ca. 1930s
Bella Lewensohn Schafer

Tapestry with Palestine monuments
Bezalel School of Arts and Crafts
Jerusalem, n.d.
Bella Lewensohn Schafer

Prayerbook with olivewood cover
Jerusalem, 1913
Rela Mintz Geffen

Photograph of Joel S. Geffen
Atlanta, Georgia, 1915
Rela Mintz Geffen

Seder plate
Bezalel School of Arts and Crafts
Jerusalem, n.d.
Rela Mintz Geffen

"Pioneer" dolls
Palestine, ca. 1940
Rela Mintz Geffen

Jerusalem landscape
dye and paint on velvet
ca. 1920s
National Museum of American Jewish History
Gift of the estate of William and Esther Lister

Silver cup
Palestine, n.d.
Minnie and Jack Miller

Photograph of Minnie and Jack Miller
Bronx, N.Y.
photoreproduction
Minnie and Jack Miller

Silver filigree bracelet
Palestine Pavilion, New York World's Fair, 1939
National Museum of American Jewish History
Purchased in memory of Ruth Alexander by Lyn M. and
George M. Ross

Advertisement for novelties
Bloch's Book Bulletin, April 1930
photoreproduction
Barbara Kirshenblatt-Gimblett

Olivewood bookholder
Palestine, n.d.
Wenger family

*Out of Doors in the Holy Land: Impressions of Travel in
Body and Spirit*
by Henry Van Dyke
New York: Charles Scribner's Sons, 1908
University of Pennsylvania Library

Tent and Saddle Life in the Holy Land
by David Van Horne
Philadelphia: American Sunday-School Union, 1886
University of Pennsylvania Library

A Springtide in Palestine by Myriam Harry
Boston and New York: Houghton Mifflin, 1924
University of Pennsylvania Library

A Pilgrimage to Palestine
by Harry Emerson Fosdick
New York: Macmillan, 1927
University of Pennsylvania Library

A Pilgrim in Palestine
by John Finley
New York: Charles Scribner's Sons, 1919
University of Pennsylvania Library

The New Mediterranean Traveler: A Handbook of Practical Information
by D. E. Lorenz
New York: Revell, 1929
University of Pennsylvania Library

Going Down from Jerusalem
by Norman Duncan
New York: Harper and Brothers, 1909
University of Pennsylvania Library

Three-dimensional Rosh Hashanah card
Germany, ca. 1910
National Museum of American Jewish History
Purchased by Elaine and Stanley Silverman in honor of "that special birthday" for Eva Schlanger

"Praying Wall at Jerusalem," advertisement for McLaughlin's Coffee
New York: Knapp Company Lithographers, 1893
Peter H. Schweitzer

Cigarette silk with Zionist Flag
Nebo cigarettes, New Jersey
early twentieth century
National Museum of American Jewish History

Cigarette silk with "Hatikvah"
early twentieth century
National Museum of American Jewish History

Studying the Holy Land

Carl Werner's Jerusalem, Bethlehem, and the Holy Places with Descriptive Letterpress by Rev. George Robert Gleig
London: Moore, McQueen & Co., 1865
Center for Judaic Studies,
University of Pennsylvania Library

The Holy Land: Drawings Made on the Spot by David Roberts with Historical Descriptions by Rev. George Croly, vol. I
London: F.G. Moon, 1842
Center for Judaic Studies,
University of Pennsylvania Library

Ordnance Survey of Jerusalem
by Captain Charles W. Wilson
London: By Authority of the Lords Commissioners of Her Majesty's Treasury, 1865
Center for Judaic Studies,
University of Pennsylvania Library

The Geography of Bible Lands
by Rena L. Crosby
New York: Abingdon Press, 1921
Center for Judaic Studies,
University of Pennsylvania Library

A Descriptive Geography and Brief Historical Sketch of Palestine
by Rabbi Joseph Schwartz, translated by Isaac Leeser
Philadelphia: A. Hart, 1850
University of Pennsylvania Library

The True Boundaries of the Holy Land
by Samuel Hillel Isaacs
Chicago: Jeanette Isaac Davis, 1917
Center for Judaic Studies,
University of Pennsylvania Library

Bible Witnesses from Bible Lands
by Robert Morris, et. al.
New York: American Holy-Land Exploration, 1874
University of Pennsylvania Library

Wood of a lemon tree
Palestine, ca. 1900
Semitic Museum, Harvard University

Wood of an orange tree
Palestine, ca. 1900
Semitic Museum, Harvard University

Bottle of straw
Palestine, ca. 1900
Semitic Museum, Harvard University

Bottle of lentils
Palestine, ca. 1900
Semitic Museum, Harvard University

Wood of a pepper tree
Palestine, ca. 1900
Semitic Museum, Harvard University

Bottle of gum arabic
Palestine, ca. 1900
Semitic Museum, Harvard University

Polished common limestone
Palestine, ca. 1900
Semitic Museum, Harvard University

Painted plaster pomegranate
Palestine, ca. 1900
Semitic Museum, Harvard University

Photograph of bird display
ca. 1903
Semitic Museum, Harvard University

Print of *salvia hierosolymitana*
Jerusalem, 1924
Ephraim Roubinovitch, artist
Center for Judaic Studies,
University of Pennsylvania Library

Flowers of the Holy Land
Jerusalem, n.d.
Center for Judaic Studies,
University of Pennsylvania Library

Photograph of archaeological excavation at Samaria
Palestine, 1908
photoreproduction
Semitic Museum, Harvard University

Excavations at Jerusalem, 1894-1897
by Frederick Jones Bliss
London: Committee of the Palestine Exploration
Fund, 1898
Center for Judaic Studies,
University of Pennsylvania Library

Ancient Synagogues in Palestine and Greece
by Eleazar L. Sukenik
London: Oxford University Press, 1934
Center for Judaic Studies,
University of Pennsylvania Library

*Recent Research in Bible Lands: Its Progress
and Results,* edited by Herman V. Hilprecht
Philadelphia: John D. Wattles & Co., 1896
Center for Judaic Studies,
University of Pennsylvania Library

The Glamour of Near East Excavation
by James Baikie
Philadelphia: J. B. Lippincott, 1923
Center for Judaic Studies,
University of Pennsylvania Library

The Archeology of Palestine and the Bible
by William Foxwell Albright
New York: Fleming H. Revell, 1932
Center for Judaic Studies,
University of Pennsylvania Library

*History of Art in Sardinia, Judaea, Syria and
Asia Minor*
by Georges Perrot and Charles Chipiez
London: Chapman and Hall, 1890
Center for Judaic Studies,
University of Pennsylvania Library

*The Four Canaanite Temples of Beth-Shan: The Temples
and Cult Objects* vol. II, part I, by Alan Rowe
Philadelphia: University of Pennsylvania Press, 1940
Center for Judaic Studies,
University of Pennsylvania Library

The Four Canaanite Temples of Beth-Shan: The Pottery
vol. II, part II, by G. M. Fitzgerald
Philadelphia: University of Pennsylvania Press, 1930
Center for Judaic Studies,
University of Pennsylvania Library

Photograph of excavation at Beth-Shan
Palestine, 1926
photoreproduction
University of Pennsylvania Museum

Photograph of group outside expedition house
Palestine, 1926
photoreproduction
University of Pennsylvania Museum

Page from field register of Beth-Shan excavation
Palestine, 1926
University of Pennsylvania Museum

Cylinder seal and impression
Late Bronze Age, found at Beth-Shan
University of Pennsylvania Museum

Unguentarium
Roman Period, found at Beth-Shan
University of Pennsylvania Museum

Grinding stone
Iron Age, found at Beth-Shan
University of Pennsylvania Museum

Pilgrim flask
Iron Age, found at Beth-Shan
University of Pennsylvania Museum

Figurine
7th-8th century B.C.E., found at Beth-Shan
University of Pennsylvania Museum

A Journalist in the Holy Land
by Arthur Copping
New York: Fleming H. Revell Co., 1912
Center for Judaic Studies,
University of Pennsylvania Library

The Living Past
by Cyrus Gordon
New York: John Day Co., 1941
Center for Judaic Studies,
University of Pennsylvania Library

Orientalisms in Bible Lands
by Edwin Wilbur Rice
Philadelphia: American Sunday-School Union, 1910
Center for Judaic Studies,
University of Pennsylvania Library

Jews in Many Lands
by Elkan Nathan Adler
Philadelphia: Jewish Publication Society of America,
1905
Center for Judaic Studies,
University of Pennsylvania Library

Photograph of tinsmith
Palestine, late 19th century
Bonfils Studio
photoreproduction
University of Pennsylvania Museum

Photograph of Syrian Jewess
Palestine, late 19th century
Bonfils Studio
photoreproduction
University of Pennsylvania Museum

Photograph of Jewish Women in Street Costume
Palestine, late 19th century
Bonfils Studio
photoreproduction
University of Pennsylvania Museum

Photograph of Rabbi in Jerusalem
Palestine, late 19th century
Bonfils Studio
photoreproduction
University of Pennsylvania Museum

Reproduction of lantern slide, "Peasant Girl
at Ramallah"
American Colony Photographers, Vester & Co.
Jerusalem, ca. 1900
Center for Judaic Studies,
University of Pennsylvania Library

Reproduction of lantern slide, "Women with their
Water Jars"
American Colony Photographers, Vester & Co.
Jerusalem, ca. 1900
Center for Judaic Studies,
University of Pennsylvania Library

Reproduction of lantern slide, "Cake and Fruit Sellers on Way to Beyrut"
American Colony Photographers, Vester & Co.
Jerusalem, ca. 1900
Center for Judaic Studies,
University of Pennsylvania Library

New Judea: Jewish Life in Modern Palestine and Egypt
by Benjamin L. Gordon
Philadelphia: Julius H. Greenstone, 1919
Center for Judaic Studies,
University of Pennsylvania Library

The Holy Land Painted by John Folleylov,
Described by John Kelman
London: Adam & Charles Black, 1912
University of Pennsylvania Library

Music of the Bible Or, Explanatory Notes Upon Those
Passages in the Sacred Scriptures Which Relate to Music
by Enoch Hutchinson
Boston: Gould and Lincoln, 1864
Center for Judaic Studies,
University of Pennsylvania Library

Plaster model of two jugs with stand
Palestine, ca. 1900
Semitic Museum, Harvard University

Plaster model of digging shovel
Palestine, ca. 1900
Semitic Museum, Harvard University

Plaster model of hammer
Palestine, ca. 1900
Semitic Museum, Harvard University

Plaster model of ax
Palestine, ca. 1900
Semitic Museum, Harvard University

Plaster model of Palestinian home
Palestine, ca. 1900
Semitic Museum, Harvard University

Flute
Palestine, ca. 1900
Semitic Museum, Harvard University

Drum with sticks
Palestine, ca. 1900
Semitic Museum, Harvard University

A Camera Crusade through the Holy Land
by Dwight L. Elmendorf
New York: Charles Scribner's Sons, 1912
Center for Judaic Studies,
University of Pennsylvania Library

Under the Flag of the Orient: A Woman's Vision of
the Master's Land
by Marion Harland
Philadelphia: Historical Publishing, 1897.
Center for Judaic Studies,
University of Pennsylvania Library

A Year's Wandering in Bible Lands
by George Aaron Barton
Philadelphia: Ferris & Leach, 1904
Center for Judaic Studies,
University of Pennsylvania Library

Those Holy Fields
by Rev. Samuel Manning
London: Religious Tract Society, 1874
Center for Judaic Studies,
University of Pennsylvania Library

Arabistan, or Land of the "Arabian Nights"
by William Perry Fogg
Hartford, Conn.: Dustin Gilman & Co., 1875
Center for Judaic Studies,
University of Pennsylvania Library

Diary of a Tour in Greece, Turkey, Egypt, and the
Holy Land vol. 2, by G. L. Dawson Damer
London: Henry Colburn, 1842
Center for Judaic Studies,
University of Pennsylvania Library

Photograph of "Climbing the Great Pyramid"
Egypt, late 19th century
Bonfils Studio
photoreproduction
Center for Judaic Studies,
University of Pennsylvania Library

Past and Present in The East
by Rev. Harry Jones
London: Religious Tract Society, 1881
Center for Judaic Studies,
University of Pennsylvania Library

Hebrew Learning Board
early 20th century
National Museum of American Jewish History
Purchased in honor of Suzanne and Norman Cohn

Photograph of boys playing baseball at Massad Hebrew Camps
ca. 1940s
photoreproduction
Rivka and Shlomo Shulsinger

The Beginner's Hebrew Self-Taught
by Philip Blackman London: R. Mazin and Co., 1935
Center for Judaic Studies,
University of Pennsylvania Library

Kadimah
Issued by the Intercollegiate Zionist
Association of America
New York: Federation of American Zionists, 1918
Center for Judaic Studies,
University of Pennsylvania Library

The Land of Promise by Edmond Fleg
New York: Macaulay, 1933
Center for Judaic Studies,
University of Pennsylvania Library

Promotional booklet
Society of Friends of "Ohel" Hebrew Dramatic Theater
ca. 1930
American Jewish Historical Society, Waltham, Mass.,
and New York, N.Y.

Promotional booklet
Palestine Hebrew Culture Fund
New York, ca. 1930s
American Jewish Historical Society, Waltham, Mass.,
and New York, N.Y.

Supporting the Holy Land

Tapestry of Theodor Herzl
Palestine, n.d.
Center for Judaic Studies,
University of Pennsylvania Library
Gift of Ruth Schechtman

Photo album of a Talmud Torah
Palestine, ca. 1940s
National Museum of American Jewish History

Broadside, General Orphan Asylum & Public Kitchens & Immigrant Home of Gallil, Palestine
New York, early twentieth century
National Museum of American Jewish History
Gift of The Anne and John P. McNulty Foundation in honor of Lyn M. and George M. Ross

Chart of enrollment, Independent Orthodox Schools of Palestine
ca. 1926
Center for Judaic Studies,
University of Pennsylvania Library

Almsbox, Hayyei Olam schools and orphanage
Jerusalem, n.d.
National Museum of American Jewish History
Purchased in honor of D. Walter Cohen by Lyn M. and George M. Ross

Certificate, United Aged Home Moshav Sekenim
Jerusalem, 1947(?)
National Museum of American Jewish History
Gift of Phyllis F. Yusem

Plaque with view of Jerusalem
Universal Yeshiva of Jerusalem
Palestine, 1943
YIVO Institute for Jewish Research Archives

Stamp, Matzoh Fund
Central Committee Knesseth Israel of Jerusalem
Palestine, n.d.
National Museum of American Jewish History

Bond certificate, Jewish Colonial Trust
1901
National Museum of American Jewish History
Gift of the children of Rubin and Rae Golden and their
families: Irv (Izzy), Joseph (Yossel), Gertrude, Francie
and Albert

Certificate, Hoachoozo Palestine Land and
Development Co.
St. Louis, Mo., 1916
Jacob Rader Marcus Center of the American Jewish
Archives, Cincinnati, Ohio

Certificate, American Zion Commonwealth
New York, 1920
National Museum of American Jewish History
In memory of Max Lekoff

Constitution, American Zion Commonwealth
New York, 1920
National Museum of American Jewish History
In memory of Max Lekoff

Stock certificate, Poale Zion Publishing Association
New York, 1920
National Museum of American Jewish History
Gift of Dina Spector

Advertisement for American Zion
Commonwealth
The New Palestine 23 June 1922
photoreproduction
Library of the Jewish Theological Seminary
of America

The Standard Map of Palestine
New York: Geographia Map Company, ca. 1947
Center for Judaic Studies,
University of Pennsylvania Library

Photograph, "Harvesting Eggplants in Nira"
United Palestine Appeal
Palestine, ca. 1940
photoreproduction
YIVO Institute for Jewish Research Archives

Photograph, "Village Industry"
United Palestine Appeal
Palestine, ca. 1940
photoreproduction
YIVO Institute for Jewish Research Archives

Photograph, "Tiller of the Good Earth"
United Palestine Appeal
Palestine, ca. 1940
photoreproduction
YIVO Institute for Jewish Research Archives

Photograph of carpenter on roof
United Palestine Appeal
Palestine, ca. 1940
photoreproduction
YIVO Institute for Jewish Research Archives

Photograph of dancers at settlement
United Palestine Appeal
Palestine, ca. 1940
photoreproduction
YIVO Institute for Jewish Research Archives

Photograph of packing oranges
United Palestine Appeal
Palestine, ca. 1940
photoreproduction
YIVO Institute for Jewish Research Archives

Booklet, "Rebuilding the Land of Israel,"
New York: United Palestine Appeal, 1926-27
National Museum of American Jewish History

Advertisements of support for Hebrew University
The New Palestine, 27 March 1925
photoreproduction
Center for Judaic Studies,
University of Pennsylvania Library

Photograph, Henrietta Szold at Hebrew
University cornerstone-laying ceremony
Jerusalem, 1934
photoreproduction
National Museum of American Jewish History

Brochure, American-Palestine Bank
Tel Aviv, 1925
Center for Judaic Studies,
University of Pennsylvania Library

Advertisement for Shemen olive oil products
Guide to New Palestine, ninth edition
Jerusalem: Benjamin Lewensohn for the Zionist
Information Bureau for Tourists in Palestine, 1936-1937
photoreproduction
Center for Judaic Studies,
University of Pennsylvania Library

Advertisement for Lubliner Palestine Cigarettes
The New Palestine, 27 March 1925
photoreproduction
Center for Judaic Studies,
University of Pennsylvania Library

Catalog, "Bezalel Exhibition: Palestine Arts
and Crafts"
New York, 1926
photoreproduction
The Jewish Museum, New York

Promised Land by Ellen Thornbecke
New York: Harper and Brothers, 1947
University of Pennsylvania Library

Photograph of Joseph Brown in Jewish Legion uniform
Palestine, ca. 1918
photoreproduction
American Jewish Historical Society, Waltham, Mass.,
and New York, N.Y.

Photograph of Jewish Legion parade
Palestine, ca. 1918
photoreproduction
American Jewish Historical Society, Waltham, Mass.,
and New York, N.Y.

United Palestine Appeal booklet
New York, 1925-26
National Museum of American Jewish History

Postcard for Fifth Zionist Congress by E.M. Lilien
Basel, Switzerland, 1901
Center for Judaic Studies,
University of Pennsylvania Library

Postcard, "Hatikvah" by E.M. Lilien
Warsaw, ca. 1900
Center for Judaic Studies,
University of Pennsylvania Library

Delegate's medal
Order Knights of Zion Convention
Chicago, 1912-1913
Hadassah, The Women's Zionist Organization
of America

Delegate's medal
Zionist Organization of America Convention
Buffalo, New York, 1936
Hadassah, The Women's Zionist Organization
of America

Certificate, Order Knights of Zion
Chicago, 1902
Hadassah, The Women's Zionist Organization of
America

Pamphlet, "Land for a Homeland"
Hadassah, ca. 1940
Hadassah, The Women's Zionist Organization of
America

Pamphlet, "Serve Palestine With the Labor
of Your Hands"
Hadassah, 1934
Hadassah, The Women's Zionist Organization of
America

Membership brochure, Bnai Zion
New York, ca. 1948
YIVO Institute for Jewish Research Archives

Photograph of 11th Young Poale Zion Convention
Syracuse, New York, 1932
photoreproduction
YIVO Institute for Jewish Research Archives

Photograph of a Poale Zion outing
early twentieth century
photoreproduction
YIVO Institute for Jewish Research Archives

Ballot for election of officers
Zionist Organization of America
North Adams, Mass., 1919
Peter H. Schweitzer

Pamphlet, "Zionism and Patriotism"
by Louis Brandeis
New York: Federation of American Zionists, 1915
National Museum of American Jewish History

Pamphlet, "Zionism vs. Judaism,"
Philadelphia: American Council for Judaism, 1944
Reform Congregation Keneseth Israel Archives

Thank-you card, "Dear American Children..."
Hadassah, 1937
Hadassah, The Women's Zionist Organization
of America

Brochure, "We Ring Your Bell Again"
Jewish National Fund, ca. 1940
Hadassah, The Women's Zionist Organization
of America

Raffle tickets, "Pile Brick on Brick Now"
Hadassah, 1938
Hadassah, The Women's Zionist Organization
of America

Tag, Zion Tag Day
Jewish National Fund, 1941
National Museum of American Jewish History
Gift of Janice Booker

Tag, Zion Tag Day
Jewish National Fund, ca. 1939
National Museum of American Jewish History
Gift of Janice Booker

Tag, Zion Tag Day
Jewish National Fund, ca. 1939
National Museum of American Jewish History
Gift of Janice Booker

Tag, Palestine Flower Day
Jewish National Fund, ca. 1939
National Museum of American Jewish History
Gift of Janice Booker

Tag, Palestine Flower Day
Jewish National Fund, ca. 1939
National Museum of American Jewish History
Gift of Janice Booker

Tag, Zion Flag Day
Jewish National Fund, ca. 1939
National Museum of American Jewish History
Gift of Janice Booker

Tag, Zion Flag Day
Jewish National Fund, 1939
National Museum of American Jewish History
Gift of Janice Booker

Tag, Zion Flag Day
Jewish National Fund, ca. 1940
National Museum of American Jewish History

Photograph of "Flower Day"
Worcester, Mass., 1914
DeDuke Studio
photoreproduction
Peter H. Schweitzer

Burlap bag for donations to Tipat Chalav
Hadassah, n.d.
Hadassah, The Women's Zionist Organization
of America

Almsbox, Jewish National Fund
ca. 1947
National Museum of American Jewish History
Purchased in memory of Arthur Poley by Lyn M. and
George M. Ross

Sheet of shekel registration coupons
New York, United States Central Shekel Board, 1939
YIVO Institute for Jewish Research Archives

Poster, "Secure a Shekel"
New York, United States Central Shekel Board, 1937
Saul Raskin, artist
photoreproduction
Judah L. Magnes Museum

Program for Anniversary Celebration
Collegiate Zionist League
New York, 1907
Peter H. Schweitzer

Banquet program
Order of the Sons of Zion
New York, 1915
YIVO Institute for Jewish Research Archives

Ticket, United Palestine Appeal Grand Zion Ball
Young Friends of Zion Club
New York, 1927
National Museum of American Jewish History
Gift of Maxine and Michael Kam

Ticket, Grand Ball of the Downtown Zionist District
New York, 1927
National Museum of American Jewish History
Gift of Maxine and Michael Kam

Ticket, Eretz Yisroel Ball
New York, 1926
National Museum of American Jewish History
Gift of Maxine and Michael Kam

Ticket, Eretz Yisroel Ball
New York, 1927
National Museum of American Jewish History
Gift of Maxine and Michael Kam

Dance Ticket, Mvasereth Zion Club
New York, 1924
National Museum of American Jewish History
Gift of Maxine and Michael Kam

Ball Ticket, Mvasereth Zion Club
New York, 1924
National Museum of American Jewish History
Gift of Maxine and Michael Kam

Photograph of Zionist March
Pittsburgh, 1919
photoreproduction
Hadassah, The Women's Zionist Organization of
America

Broadside, "Monster Protest Meeting"
Boston, 1930
National Museum of American Jewish History
Gift of The Anne and John P. McNulty Foundation in
honor of Lyn M. and George M. Ross

Poster, Palestine Maccabees vs. Pennsylvania All Stars
Philadelphia, 1936
Peter H. Schweitzer

**Program, June Night Frolic for Palestine Land
Redemption**
New York, 1935
YIVO Institute for Jewish Research Library

Poster, lecture by Stephen Wise
New Hampshire, 1938
Peter H. Schweitzer

Program, Annual Third Seder Festival
Zionist Organization of America
Atlantic City, New Jersey, 1939
YIVO Institute for Jewish Research Library

Advertisement for Zionist flags
The New Palestine, 27 March 1925
Center for Judaic Studies,
University of Pennsylvania Library

Advertisement for Herzl penknife
The New Palestine, 16 June 1922
Library of the Jewish Theological Seminary of
America

Tree Planting Certificate
Jewish National Fund, 1936
Hadassah, The Women's Zionist Organization of
America

Tree Planting Certificate
Jewish National Fund, 1945
National Museum of American Jewish History
Gift of Lillian Linden

Jewish National Fund Certificate
Congregation Agudat Achim, Philadelphia, 1946
National Museum of American Jewish History
Gift of Clara K. Braslow, in memory of her parents

Pin, Palestine Lunch Fund
Hadassah, n.d.
National Museum of American Jewish History
Purchased in honor of Bubbles Seidenberg by Margo
Bloom

Pin in shape of nurse's hat
Hadassah, n.d.
National Museum of American Jewish History

Pin, Hadassah life member
Hadassah, n.d.
National Museum of American Jewish History

Pin, Junior Hadassah
Hadassah, n.d.
National Museum of American Jewish History

Pin, Hadassah associates
Hadassah, n.d.
National Museum of American Jewish History

Matchbook, Zionist Organization of America
ca. 1947
National Museum of American Jewish History

Set of five metal ashtrays
Jewish National Fund, n.d.
National Museum of American Jewish History

Booklet of stamps
Jewish National Fund, 1919
National Museum of American Jewish History

Stamps of Chaim Weizmann
Jewish National Fund, 1944
National Museum of American Jewish History

Stamp of ship
Jerusalem: Jewish National Fund, n.d.
National Museum of American Jewish History

Bookmark, "Purim Greetings"
Jewish National Fund
Peter H. Schweitzer

Epilogue: From Palestine to Israel

Commemorative plate
Newark, New Jersey: Stores Inc., 1948
National Museum of American Jewish History

Tree Planting Certificate: "Forest of 6,000,000"
New York, Jewish National Fund Council of Hadassah,
n.d.
Peter H. Schweitzer

Paper almsbox
Jewish National Fund, n.d.
National Museum of American Jewish History
Gift of David Zipkin

Button, "Zionism is a Badge of Honor"
Zionist Organization of America
National Museum of American Jewish History

Button, "I love Israel"
(in Hebrew)
National Museum of American Jewish History
Gift of Rebecca Lillian

**Button, "Kahana
in Knesset"**
National Museum of American Jewish History

Button, "Two peoples, two states"
National Museum of American Jewish History

Button, "Shalom"
National Museum of American Jewish History

Button, Pioneer Women
National Museum of American Jewish History

Film poster, *Exodus,* directed by Otto Preminger
United Artists, 1960
Peter H. Schweitzer

Catalog, Magold Company Israel Creations
Philadelphia, ca. 1960s
National Museum of American Jewish History

Copper Israel ashtray
Peter H. Schweitzer

Set of six Chagall coasters
Peter H. Schweitzer

Advertisement for Israeli stamps
Gimbels Stamp News, August 1948
Peter H. Schweitzer

Jigsaw puzzle of Israel
Peter H. Schweitzer

Record set, "Living Hebrew"
New York: Living Language Courses, 1958
Jeffrey Shandler

Playing cards
El Al Airlines, ca. 1970
Jeffrey Shandler

Hat with portrait of Moshe Dayan
Israel, 1968
Harold and Judith Einhorn

T-shirt, Coca-Cola in Hebrew
Beth S. Wenger

Viewmaster and Disks of Holy Land
Portland, Oregon, 1951
Visual Collections, Fine Arts Library, Harvard University

Photograph of International Jewish Arts Festival,
Suffolk Y Jewish Community Center
Commack, Long Island, New York, 1995
Copyright, Frédéric Brenner
Courtesy Howard Greenberg Gallery, New York

List of Lenders

American Jewish Historical Society,
Waltham, Massachusetts and New York, N.Y.

Center for Judaic Studies,
University of Pennsylvania Library, Philadelphia

Central Zionist Archives, Jerusalem

Chautauqua Institution Archives,
Chautauqua, New York

Dr. Ierach and Dalia Daskal, Philadelphia

Harold and Judith Einhorn

Stanley D. and Elaine L. Ferst, Philadelphia

Fine Arts Library, Harvard University,
Cambridge, Massachusetts

Rela Mintz Geffen, Philadelphia

Howard Greenberg Gallery, New York

Hadassah, The Women's Zionist
Organization of America, New York

The Jewish Museum, New York

Library of the Jewish Theological
Seminary of America, New York

Barbara Kirshenblatt-Gimblett, New York

Library of Congress, Washington, D.C.

Judah L. Magnes Museum, Berkeley, California

Jacob Rader Marcus Center of the American
Jewish Archives, Cincinnati, Ohio

Jack and Minnie Singer Miller, New York

National Center for Jewish Film,
Waltham, Massachusetts

National Museum of American Jewish History,
Philadelphia

92nd Street YM/YWHA Archives, New York

Isaac Pollak, New York

Joseph and Miriam Ratner Center for the Study of
Conservative Judaism, Jewish Theological
Seminary of America, New York

Reform Congregation Keneseth Israel Archives,
Philadelphia

Bella Lewensohn Schafer, Philadelphia

Peter H. Schweitzer, New York

Semitic Museum, Harvard University,
Cambridge, Massachusetts

Jeffrey Shandler, New York

Rivka and Shlomo Shulsinger, Jerusalem

Tuttleman Library of Gratz College, Philadelphia

University of Pennsylvania Library, Philadelphia

University of Pennsylvania Museum, Philadelphia

Weill-Lenya Research Center, Kurt Weill Foundation for
Music, New York

Weizmann Institute of Science, Rehovot, Israel

Beth Wenger, Philadelphia

Wenger family, Atlanta, Georgia

Yale University Library, New Haven, Connecticut

YIVO Institute for Jewish Research, New York